Instruction on the Eucharist

Redemptionis Sacramentum

*On Certain Matters to Be Observed or
to Be Avoided Regarding the Most Holy Eucharist*

LITURGY DOCUMENTARY SERIES 15

United States Conference of Catholic Bishops • Washington, D.C.

Concordat cum originali:
Msgr. James Patrick Moroney
Executive Director, Secretariat for the Liturgy
United States Conference of Catholic Bishops

Publication No. 5-619
USCCB Publishing
Washington, D.C.
ISBN 1-57455-619-3

Text from the
CONGREGATION FOR DIVINE WORSHIP AND
THE DISCIPLINE OF THE SACRAMENTS
Vatican City

Published in the United States, May 2004

Contents

CHAPTER VIII

CONGREGATION FOR DIVINE WORSHIP
AND THE DISCIPLINE OF THE SACRAMENTS

INTRODUCTION TO THE USCCB EDITION

"The most blessed Eucharist contains the Church's entire spiritual wealth, that is, Christ himself, our passover and living bread," says the Second Vatican Council (*Presbyterorum Ordinis*, no. 5). The Eucharistic Sacrifice, the sacramental representation of the Sacrifice of the Cross is "the fount and apex of the whole Christian life" (*Lumen Gentium*, no. 11). The Eucharist, the sacrament of the Paschal Mystery of the suffering, death, and resurrection of Christ, "stands at the center of the Church's life" (John Paul II, *Ecclesia de Eucharistia*, no. 3).

It is therefore no surprise that all along the centuries the Church has surrounded the celebration of this mystery of faith with reverence, care, devotion, and love. This is the reason for liturgical norms concerning the celebration, reception, and adoration of the Holy Eucharist. This mystery "is too great for anyone to feel free to treat it lightly and with disregard for its sacredness and its universality" (*Ecclesia de Eucharistia*, no. 52).

These are the reasons for this *Instruction*, which the Congregation for Divine Worship and the Discipline of the Sacraments would like to put into the hands of every cleric, religious, and member of the lay faithful.

I congratulate the Publications Department of the United States Conference of Catholic Bishops for its initiative in having this *Instruction* published and distributed in the country and wish it God's abundant blessing.

Francis Cardinal Arinze
Prefect
April 23, 2004

Introduction

1. ORIGINS OF THIS INSTRUCTION

It helps first of all to place this *Instruction* at its origins. At the Solemn Last Supper Mass on Holy Thursday in St Peter's Basilica, on April 17, 2003, the Holy Father signed and gave to the Church his fourteenth encyclical letter, *Ecclesia de Eucharistia.*

In this beautiful document Pope John Paul II states, *inter alia*, that the Holy Eucharist "stands at the center of the Church's life" (no. 3), that "it unites heaven and earth. It embraces and permeates all creation" (no. 8), and that it "is the most precious possession which the Church can have in her journey through history" (no. 9).

At the same time he notes that there are positive and negative developments in its celebration and worship since the Second Vatican Council (no. 10), that a number of abuses have been a source of suffering for many and that he considers it his duty "to appeal urgently that the liturgical norms for the celebration of the Eucharist be observed with great fidelity" (no. 52). "Precisely to bring out more clearly this deeper meaning of liturgical norms," he continued, "I have asked the competent offices of the Roman Curia to prepare a more specific document, including prescriptions of a juridical nature, on this very important subject. No one is permitted to undervalue the mystery entrusted to our hands: it is too great for anyone to feel free to treat it lightly and with disregard for its sacredness and its universality" (no. 52).

This is the origin of this *Instruction* which the Congregation for Divine Worship and the Discipline of the Sacraments, in close collaboration with the Congregation for the Doctrine of the Faith, now offers to the Latin Church.

2. REASONS FOR LITURGICAL NORMS

Someone may ask why there should be liturgical norms at all. Would creativity, spontaneity, the freedom of the children of God and ordinary good sense not be enough? Why should the worship of God be regimented by rubrics and regulations? Is it not enough just to teach people the beauty and the exalted nature of the Liturgy?

Liturgical norms are necessary because "in liturgy full public worship is performed by the Mystical Body of Jesus Christ, that is, by the Head and by his members. From this it follows that every liturgical celebration, because it is an action of Christ the priest and of his Body the Church, is a sacred action surpassing all others" (*Sacrosanctum Concilium*, no. 7). And the summit of the Liturgy is the Eucharistic celebration. No one should be surprised if, with the passage of time, Holy Mother Church has developed words and actions, and therefore directives, for this supreme act of worship. Eucharistic norms are devised to express and protect the Eucharistic mystery and also manifest that it is the Church that celebrates this august sacrifice and Sacrament. As Pope John Paul II puts it, "These norms are a concrete expression of the authentically ecclesial nature of the Eucharist; this is their deepest meaning. Liturgy is never anyone's private property, be it of the celebrant or of the community in which the mysteries are celebrated" (*Ecclesia de Eucharistia*, no. 52).

It follows that "priests who faithfully celebrate Mass according to the liturgical norms, and communities which conform to these norms, quietly but eloquently demonstrate their love for the Church" (ibid.).

Obviously, external conformity is not enough. Faith, hope and charity, which also manifest themselves in acts of solidarity with the needy, are demanded by participation in the Holy Eucharist. This *Instruction* underlines this dimension in article 5: "A merely external observation of norms would obviously be contrary to the nature of the sacred Liturgy, in which Christ himself wishes to gather his Church, so that together with himself she will be 'one body and one spirit.' For this reason, external action must be illuminated by faith and charity which unite us with Christ and with one another and engender love for the poor and the abandoned."

3. IS IT IMPORTANT TO PAY ATTENTION TO ABUSES?

An allied temptation which has to be resisted is that it is a waste of time to pay attention to liturgical abuses. Someone wrote that abuses always existed and always will exist, and that therefore we should just get on with positive liturgical formation and celebration.

This objection, true in part, can be rather misleading. All abuses regarding the Holy Eucharist are not of the same weight. Some threaten to make the Sacrament invalid. Some are manifestations of deficiency in Eucharistic faith. Others contribute to confusion among the People of God and to growing desacralization of Eucharistic celebrations. They are not banal.

Of course liturgical formation is necessary for all in the Church. "It is vitally necessary," says the Second Vatican Council, "that attention be directed, above all, to the liturgical instruction of the clergy" (*Sacrosanctum Concilium*, no. 14). But it is also true that "in various parts of the Church abuses have occurred, leading to confusion with regard to sound faith and Catholic doctrine concerning this wonderful sacrament" (*Ecclesia de Eucharistia*, no. 10). "Not infrequently, abuses are rooted in a false understanding of liberty" (*Instruction on the Eucharist*, no. 7). "Arbitrary actions are not conducive to true renewal" (*Instruction*, no. 11) for which the Second Vatican Council hoped. "These abuses have nothing to do with the authentic spirit of the Council and must be prudently and firmly corrected by Pastors" (John Paul II: Letter on Fortieth Anniversary of Sacrosanctum Concilium, *Spiritus et Sponsa*, no. 15).

As for those who modify liturgical texts on their own authority, it is important to observe with this *Instruction* that "the sacred Liturgy is quite intimately connected with principles of doctrine, so that the use of unapproved texts and rites necessarily leads either to the diminution or to the elimination of that necessary link between the *lex orandi* and the *lex credendi*" (*Instruction*, no. 10).

4. OVERVIEW OF THE INSTRUCTION

The *Instruction* has an introduction, eight chapters, and a conclusion.

The first chapter, on the regulation of the Sacred Liturgy, speaks of the roles of the Apostolic See, the diocesan Bishop, the Bishops' Conference, Priests and Deacons. I single out the role of the diocesan Bishop. He is the high priest of his flock. He directs, encourages, promotes and organizes. He looks into sacred music and art. He sets up needed commissions for Liturgy, music and sacred art (*Instruction*, nos. 22, 25). He seeks remedies for abuses and it is to him or his assistants that recourse should first be made rather than to the Apostolic See (*Instruction*, nos. 176-182, 184).

Priests have also made solemn promises to exercise with fidelity their ministry, as have Deacons. They are expected to live up to their sacred responsibilities.

The second chapter concentrates on the participation of the lay faithful in the Eucharistic celebration. Baptism is the foundation for the common priesthood (*Instruction*, nos. 36, 37). The ordained Priest remains indispensable for a Christian community and the roles of the Priests and of the lay faithful should not be confused (*Instruction*, nos. 42, 45). Laypeople have their proper role. The *Instruction* stresses that this does not mean that everybody has to be doing something. Rather it is a question of being fully alive to the great privilege that God has given them in calling them to participate with mind and heart and their entire life in the Liturgy and through it to receive God's grace. It is important to understand this properly and not to suppose that the *Instruction* is somehow biased against laypeople.

Chapters 3, 4 and 5 seek to answer some of the questions sometimes asked and to address some known abuses regarding the actual Mass celebration, discernment on who receives Holy Communion and who should not, care required for Holy Communion under two forms, and questions regarding sacred vestments and vessels, posture while receiving Holy Communion, and such like.

Chapter 6 is on worship of the Holy Eucharist outside Mass. It treats of due respect for the tabernacle, and practices such as visits to the Blessed Sacrament, Perpetual Adoration Chapel, and Eucharistic Processions and Congresses (*Instruction*, nos. 130, 135-136, 140, 142-145).

Chapter 7 gives attention to extraordinary offices entrusted to the lay faithful, such as those of extraordinary ministers of Holy Communion, instructors or leaders of prayer services in the absence of a Priest (*Instruction*, nos. 147-169). These roles are different from what the *Instruction* speaks of in Chapter 2, where it talks of the ordinary participation of laypeople in the Liturgy, and in particular in the Eucharist. Here it is a question of the things that laypeople are called upon to do when sufficient Priests or even Deacons are not available. The Holy See has paid considerable attention to this question in recent years and this *Instruction* follows suit, adding further considerations for certain circumstances.

The final chapter is on canonical remedies for crimes or abuses against the Holy Eucharist. The main remedy in the long term is proper formation and instruction and sound faith. But when abuses do occur, the Church has a duty to address them in a clear and charitable way.

5. CONCLUSION

In view of the article of faith that the Mass is a sacramental representation of the Sacrifice of the Cross (cf. Council of Trent: DS 1740) and that in the Most Blessed Sacrament of the Eucharist "the body and blood, together with the soul and divinity, of our Lord Jesus Christ and, therefore, the whole Christ is truly, really and substantially contained" (Council of Trent: DS 1651; cf. *Catechism of the Catholic Church*, no. 1374), it is clear that liturgical norms regarding the Holy Eucharist deserve our attention. They are not meticulous rubrics dictated by legalistically bent minds.

"The most blessed Eucharist contains the Church's entire spiritual wealth, that is, Christ himself, our passover and living bread" (*Presbyterorum Ordinis*, no. 5). Priests and Bishops are ordained above all to celebrate the Eucharistic sacrifice and give the Body and Blood of Christ to the faithful. Deacons and, in their own ways, acolytes, other servers, lectors and choirs and specially deputed lay faithful are recalled to assist in definite functions. They should all in faith and devotion strive to discharge their various ministries.

The *Instruction* therefore concludes that the Congregation for Divine Worship and the Discipline of the Sacraments hopes that "by the diligent application of those things that are called in this *Instruction*, human weakness may come to pose less of an obstacle to the action of the Most Holy Sacrament of the Eucharist, and that with all distortion set aside and every reprobated practice removed, through the intercession of the Blessed Virgin Mary, 'Woman of the Eucharist,' the saving presence of Christ in the Sacrament of his Body and Blood may shine brightly upon all people" (*Instruction*, no. 185).

Francis Cardinal Arinze
April 23, 2004

INSTRUCTION ON THE EUCHARIST

Redemptionis Sacramentum

On Certain Matters to Be Observed or
to Be Avoided Regarding the Most Holy Eucharist

Preamble

1. In the Most Holy Eucharist, Mother Church with steadfast faith acknowledges the SACRAMENT OF REDEMPTION,[1] joyfully takes it to herself, celebrates it and reveres it in adoration, proclaiming the death of Christ Jesus and confessing his Resurrection until he comes in glory[2] to hand over, as unconquered Lord and Ruler, eternal Priest and King of the Universe, a kingdom of truth and life to the immense majesty of the Almighty Father.[3]

2. The Church's doctrine regarding the Most Holy Eucharist, in which the whole spiritual wealth of the Church is contained—namely Christ, our Paschal Lamb[4]—the Eucharist which is the source and summit of the whole of Christian life,[5] and which lies as a causative force behind the very origins of the Church,[6] has been expounded with thoughtful care and with great authority over the course of the centuries in the writings of the Councils and the Supreme Pontiffs. Most recently, in fact, the Supreme Pontiff John Paul II, in the Encyclical Letter *Ecclesia*

---

1   Cf. MISSALE ROMANUM, ex decreto sacrosancti Oecumenici Concilii Vaticani II instauratum, auctoritate Pauli Pp. VI promulgatum, Ioannis Pauli Pp. II cura recognitum, editio typica tertia, 20 April 2000, Typis Vaticanis, 2002, Missa votiva de Dei misericordia, oratio super oblata, p. 1159.

2   Cf. 1 Cor 11:26; MISSALE ROMANUM, Prex Eucharistica, acclamatio post consecrationem, p. 576; POPE JOHN PAUL II, Encyclical Letter, *Ecclesia de Eucharistia*, 17 April 2003, nos. 5, 11, 14, 18: AAS 95 (2003) pp. 436, 440-441, 442, 445.

3   Cf. Is 10:33; 51:22; MISSALE ROMANUM, In sollemnitate Domini nostri Iesu Christi, universorum Regis, Praefatio, p. 499.

4   Cf. 1 Cor 5:7; SECOND VATICAN ECUMENICAL COUNCIL, Decree on the Ministry and Life of Priests, *Presbyterorum ordinis*, 7 December 1965, no. 5; POPE JOHN PAUL II, Apostolic Exhortation, *Ecclesia in Europa*, no. 75: AAS 95 (2003) pp. 649-719, here p. 693.

5   Cf. SECOND VATICAN ECUMENICAL COUNCIL, Dogmatic Constitution on the Church, *Lumen gentium*, 21 November 1964, no. 11.

6   Cf. POPE JOHN PAUL II, Encyclical Letter, *Ecclesia de Eucharistia*, 17 April 2003, no. 21: AAS 95 (2003) p. 447.

de Eucharistia, set forth afresh certain elements of great importance on this subject in view of the ecclesial circumstances of our times.[7]

In order that especially in the celebration of the Sacred Liturgy the Church might duly safeguard so great a mystery in our own time as well, the Supreme Pontiff has mandated that this Congregation for Divine Worship and the Discipline of the Sacraments,[8] in collaboration with the Congregation for the Doctrine of the Faith, should prepare this Instruction treating of certain matters pertaining to the discipline of the Sacrament of the Eucharist. Those things found in this Instruction are therefore to be read in the continuity with the above-mentioned Encyclical Letter, *Ecclesia de Eucharistia.*

It is not at all the intention here to prepare a compendium of the norms regarding the Most Holy Eucharist, but rather, to take up within this Instruction some elements of liturgical norms that have been previously expounded or laid down and even today remain in force in order to ensure a deeper appreciation of the liturgical norms;[9] to establish certain norms by which those earlier ones are explained and complemented; and also to set forth for Bishops, as well as for Priests, Deacons and all the lay Christian faithful, how each should carry them out in accordance with his own responsibilities and the means at his disposal.

3. The norms contained in the present Instruction are to be understood as pertaining to liturgical matters in the Roman Rite, and, *mutatis mutandis,* in the other Rites of the Latin Church that are duly acknowledged by law.

4. "Certainly the liturgical reform inaugurated by the Council has greatly contributed to a more conscious, active and fruitful participation

---

7   Ibid.: AAS 95 (2003) pp. 433-475.
8   Ibid., no. 52: AAS 95 (2003) p. 468.
9   Ibid.

4

in the Holy Sacrifice of the Altar on the part of the faithful."[10] Even so, "shadows are not lacking."[11] In this regard it is not possible to be silent about the abuses, even quite grave ones, against the nature of the Liturgy and the Sacraments as well as the tradition and the authority of the Church, which in our day not infrequently plague liturgical celebrations in one ecclesial environment or another. In some places the perpetration of liturgical abuses has become almost habitual, a fact which obviously cannot be allowed and must cease.

5. The observance of the norms published by the authority of the Church requires conformity of thought and of word, of external action and of the application of the heart. A merely external observation of norms would obviously be contrary to the nature of the Sacred Liturgy, in which Christ himself wishes to gather his Church, so that together with himself she will be "one body and one spirit."[12] For this reason, external action must be illuminated by faith and charity, which unite us with Christ and with one another and engender love for the poor and the abandoned. The liturgical words and Rites, moreover, are a faithful expression, matured over the centuries, of the understanding of Christ, and they teach us to think as he himself does;[13] by conforming our minds to these words, we raise our hearts to the Lord. All that is said in this Instruction is directed toward such a conformity of our own understanding with that of Christ, as expressed in the words and the Rites of the Liturgy.

6. For abuses "contribute to the obscuring of the Catholic faith and doctrine concerning this wonderful sacrament."[14] Thus, they also hinder

---

10   Ibid., no. 10: AAS 95 (2003) p. 439.
11   Ibid.; cf. POPE JOHN PAUL II, Apostolic Letter, *Vicesimus quintus annus*, 4 December 1988, nos. 12-13: AAS 81 (1989) pp. 909-910; cf. also SECOND VATICAN ECUMENICAL COUNCIL, Constitution on the Sacred Liturgy, *Sacrosanctum Concilium*, 4 December 1963, no. 48.
12   MISSALE ROMANUM, Prex Eucharistica III, p. 588; cf. 1 Cor 12:12-13; Eph 4:4.
13   Cf. Phil 2:5.
14   POPE JOHN PAUL II, Encyclical Letter, *Ecclesia de Eucharistia*, no. 10: AAS 95 (2003) p. 439.

the faithful from "re-living in a certain way the experience of the two disciples of Emmaus: 'and their eyes were opened, and they recognized him.'"[15] For in the presence of God's power and divinity[16] and the splendor of his goodness, made manifest especially in the Sacrament of the Eucharist, it is fitting that all the faithful should have and put into practice that power of acknowledging God's majesty that they have received through the saving Passion of the Only-Begotten Son.[17]

7. Not infrequently, abuses are rooted in a false understanding of liberty. Yet God has not granted us in Christ an illusory liberty by which we may do what we wish, but a liberty by which we may do that which is fitting and right.[18] This is true not only of precepts coming directly from God, but also of laws promulgated by the Church, with appropriate regard for the nature of each norm. For this reason, all should conform to the ordinances set forth by legitimate ecclesiastical authority.

8. It is therefore to be noted with great sadness that "ecumenical initiatives which are well-intentioned, nevertheless indulge at times in Eucharistic practices contrary to the discipline by which the Church expresses her faith." Yet the Eucharist "is too great a gift to tolerate ambiguity or depreciation." It is therefore necessary that some things be corrected or more clearly delineated so that in this respect as well "the Eucharist will continue to shine forth in all its radiant mystery."[19]

---

15   Ibid., no. 6: AAS 95 (2003) p. 437; cf. Lk 24:31.
16   Cf. Rom 1:20.
17   Cf. MISSALE ROMANUM, Praefatio I de Passione Domini, p. 528.
18   Cf. POPE JOHN PAUL II, Encyclical Letter, *Veritatis splendor*, 6 August 1993, no. 35: AAS 85 (1993) pp. 1161-1162; Homily given at Camden Yards, 9 October 1995, no. 7: *Insegnamenti di Giovanni Paolo II*, XVII, 2 (1995), Libreria Editrice Vaticana, 1998, p. 788.
19   Cf. POPE JOHN PAUL II, Encyclical Letter, *Ecclesia de Eucharistia*, no. 10: AAS 95 (2003) p. 439.

9. Finally, abuses are often based on ignorance, in that they involve a rejection of those elements whose deeper meaning is not understood and whose antiquity is not recognized. For "the liturgical prayers, orations and songs are pervaded by the inspiration and impulse" of the Sacred Scriptures themselves, "and it is from these that the actions and signs receive their meaning."[20] As for the visible signs "which the Sacred Liturgy uses in order to signify the invisible divine realities, they have been chosen by Christ or by the Church."[21] Finally, the structures and forms of the sacred celebrations according to each of the Rites of both East and West are in harmony with the practice of the universal Church also as regards practices received universally from apostolic and unbroken tradition,[22] which it is the Church's task to transmit faithfully and carefully to future generations. All these things are wisely safeguarded and protected by the liturgical norms.

10. The Church herself has no power over those things which were established by Christ himself and which constitute an unchangeable part of the Liturgy.[23] Indeed, if the bond were to be broken which the

---

20   SECOND VATICAN ECUMENICAL COUNCIL, Constitution on the Sacred Liturgy, *Sacrosanctum Concilium*, no. 24; cf. CONGREGATION FOR DIVINE WORSHIP AND THE DISCIPLINE OF THE SACRAMENTS, Instruction, *Varietates legitimae*, 25 January 1994, nos. 19, 23: AAS 87 (1995) pp. 295-296, 297.

21   SECOND VATICAN ECUMENICAL COUNCIL, Constitution on the Sacred Liturgy, *Sacrosanctum Concilium*, no. 33.

22   Cf. ST. IRENAEUS, *Adversus Haereses*, III, 2: SCh.., 211, 24-31; ST. AUGUSTINE, *Epistula ad Ianuarium*: 54,I: PL 33,200: *"Illa autem quae non scripta, sed tradita custodimus, quae quidem toto terrarum orbe servantur, datur intellegi vel ab ipsis Apostolis, vel plenariis conciliis, quorum est Ecclesia saluberrima auctoritas, commendata atque statuta retineri"*; POPE JOHN PAUL II, Encyclical Letter, *Redemptoris missio*, 7 December 1990, nos. 53-54: AAS 83 (1991) pp. 300-302; CONGREGATION FOR THE DOCTRINE OF THE FAITH, Letter to the Bishops of the Catholic Church on Certain Aspects of the Church as Communion, *Communionis notio*, 28 May 1992, nos. 7-10: AAS 85 (1993) pp. 842-844; CONGREGATION FOR DIVINE WORSHIP AND THE DISCIPLINE OF THE SACRAMENTS, Instruction, *Varietates legitimae*, no. 26: AAS 87 (1995) pp. 298-299.

23   Cf. SECOND VATICAN ECUMENICAL COUNCIL, Constitution on the Sacred Liturgy, *Sacrosanctum Concilium*, no. 21.

Sacraments have with Christ himself who instituted them, and with the events of the Church's founding,[24] it would not be beneficial to the faithful but rather would do them grave harm. For the Sacred Liturgy is quite intimately connected with principles of doctrine,[25] so that the use of unapproved texts and Rites necessarily leads either to the attenuation or to the disappearance of that necessary link between the *lex orandi* and the *lex credendi*.[26]

11. The Mystery of the Eucharist "is too great for anyone to permit himself to treat it according to his own whim, so that its sacredness and its universal ordering would be obscured."[27] On the contrary, anyone who acts thus by giving free reign to his own inclinations, even if he is a Priest, injures the substantial unity of the Roman Rite, which ought to be vigorously preserved,[28] and becomes responsible for actions that are in no way consistent with the hunger and thirst for the living God that is experienced by the people today. Nor do such actions serve authentic pastoral care or proper liturgical renewal; instead, they

---

24 Cf. POPE PIUS XII, Apostolic Constitution, *Sacramentum Ordinis*, 30 November 1947: AAS 40 (1948) p. 5; CONGREGATION FOR THE DOCTRINE OF THE FAITH, Declaration, *Inter insigniores*, 15 October 1976, part IV: AAS 69 (1977) pp. 107-108; CONGREGATION FOR DIVINE WORSHIP AND THE DISCIPLINE OF THE SACRAMENTS, Instruction, *Varietates legitimae*, no. 25: AAS 87 (1995) p. 298.

25 Cf. POPE PIUS XII, Encyclical Letter, *Mediator Dei*, 20 November 1947: AAS 39 (1947) p. 540.

26 Cf. S. CONGREGATION FOR THE SACRAMENTS AND DIVINE WORSHIP, Instruction, *Inaestimabile donum*, 3 April 1980: AAS 72 (1980) p. 333.

27 POPE JOHN PAUL II, Encyclical Letter, *Ecclesia de Eucharistia*, no. 52: AAS 95 (2003) p. 468.

28 SECOND VATICAN ECUMENICAL COUNCIL, Constitution on the Sacred Liturgy, *Sacrosanctum Concilium*, nos. 4, 38; Decree on the Catholic Eastern Churches, *Orientalium Ecclesiarum*, 21 November 1964, nos. 1, 2, 6; POPE PAUL VI, Apostolic Constitution, *Missale Romanum*: AAS 61 (1969) pp. 217-222; MISSALE ROMANUM, Institutio Generalis, no. 399; CONGREGATION FOR DIVINE WORSHIP AND THE DISCIPLINE OF THE SACRAMENTS, Instruction, *Liturgiam authenticam*, 28 March 2001, no. 4: AAS 93 (2001) pp. 685-726, here p. 686.

deprive Christ's faithful of their patrimony and their heritage. For arbitrary actions are not conducive to true renewal,[29] but are detrimental to the right of Christ's faithful to a liturgical celebration that is an expression of the Church's life in accordance with her tradition and discipline. In the end, they introduce elements of distortion and disharmony into the very celebration of the Eucharist, which is oriented in its own lofty way and by its very nature to signifying and wondrously bringing about the communion of divine life and the unity of the People of God.[30] The result is uncertainty in matters of doctrine, perplexity and scandal on the part of the People of God, and, almost as a necessary consequence, vigorous opposition, all of which greatly confuse and sadden many of Christ's faithful in this age of ours when Christian life is often particularly difficult on account of the inroads of "secularization" as well.[31]

12. On the contrary, it is the right of all of Christ's faithful that the Liturgy, and in particular the celebration of Holy Mass, should truly be as the Church wishes, according to her stipulations as prescribed in the liturgical books and in the other laws and norms. Likewise, the Catholic people have the right that the Sacrifice of the Holy Mass should be celebrated for them in an integral manner, according to the entire doctrine of the Church's Magisterium. Finally, it is the Catholic community's right that the celebration of the Most Holy Eucharist should be carried out for it in such a manner that it truly stands out as

---

29   Cf. POPE JOHN PAUL II, Apostolic Exhortation, *Ecclesia in Europa*, no. 72: AAS 95 (2003).

30   Cf. POPE JOHN PAUL II, Encyclical Letter, *Ecclesia de Eucharistia*, no. 23: AAS 95 (2003) pp. 448-449; S. CONGREGATION OF RITES, Instruction, *Eucharisticum mysterium*, 25 May 1967, no. 6: AAS 59 (1967) p. 545.

31   S. CONGREGATION FOR THE SACRAMENTS AND DIVINE WORSHIP, Instruction, *Inaestimabile donum*: AAS 72 (1980) pp. 332-333.

a sacrament of unity, to the exclusion of all blemishes and actions that might engender divisions and factions in the Church.[32]

13. All of the norms and exhortations set forth in this Instruction are connected, albeit in various ways, with the mission of the Church, whose task it is to be vigilant concerning the correct and worthy cele-bration of so great a mystery. The last chapter of the present Instruction will treat of the varying degrees to which the individual norms are bound up with the supreme norm of all ecclesiastical law, namely concern for the salvation of souls.[33]

---

32   Cf. 1 Cor 11:17-34; POPE JOHN PAUL II, Encyclical Letter, *Ecclesia de Eucharistia*, no. 52: AAS 95 (2003) pp. 467-468.

33   Cf. *Code of C anon Law*, 25 January 1983, can. 1752.

CHAPTER I
The Regulation of the
Sacred Liturgy

14. "The regulation of the Sacred Liturgy depends solely on the authority of the Church, which rests specifically with the Apostolic See and, according to the norms of law, with the Bishop.[34]

15. The Roman Pontiff, "the Vicar of Christ and the Pastor of the universal Church on earth, by virtue of his supreme office enjoys full, immediate and universal ordinary power, which he may always freely exercise,"[35] also by means of communication with the pastors and with the members of the flock.

16. "It pertains to the Apostolic See to regulate the Sacred Liturgy of the universal Church, to publish the liturgical books and to grant the *recognitio* for their translation into vernacular languages, as well as to ensure that the liturgical regulations, especially those governing the celebration of the most exalted celebration of the Sacrifice of the Mass, are everywhere faithfully observed."[36]

17. "The Congregation for Divine Worship and the Discipline of the Sacraments attends to those matters that pertain to the Apostolic See as regards the regulation and promotion of the Sacred Liturgy, and especially the Sacraments, with due regard for the competence of the

---

34   SECOND VATICAN ECUMENICAL COUNCIL, Constitution on the Sacred Liturgy, *Sacrosanctum Concilium*, no. 22 §1; cf. *Code of Canon Law*, can. 838 §1.

35   *Code of Canon Law*, can. 331; cf. SECOND VATICAN ECUMENICAL COUNCIL, Dogmatic Constitution on the Church, *Lumen gentium*, no. 22.

36   *Code of Canon Law*, can. 838 §2.

Congregation for the Doctrine of the Faith. It fosters and enforces sacramental discipline, especially as regards their validity and their licit celebration." Finally, it "carefully seeks to ensure that the liturgical regulations are observed with precision, and that abuses are prevented or eliminated whenever they are detected."[37] In this regard, according to the tradition of the universal Church, pre-eminent solicitude is accorded the celebration of Holy Mass, and also to the worship that is given to the Holy Eucharist even outside Mass.

18. Christ's faithful have the right that ecclesiastical authority should fully and efficaciously regulate the Sacred Liturgy lest it should ever seem to be "anyone's private property, whether of the celebrant or of the community in which the mysteries are celebrated."[38]

1. THE DIOCESAN BISHOP, HIGH PRIEST OF HIS FLOCK

19. The diocesan Bishop, the first steward of the mysteries of God in the particular Church entrusted to him, is the moderator, promoter and guardian of her whole liturgical life.[39] For "the Bishop, endowed with the fullness of the Sacrament of Order, is 'the steward of the grace of the high Priesthood,'[40] especially in the Eucharist which he either himself offers or causes to be offered,[41] by which the Church continually lives and grows."[42]

---

37   Cf. POPE JOHN PAUL II, Apostolic Constitution, *Pastor bonus*, 28 June 1988: AAS 80 (1988) pp. 841-924, here articles. 62, 63, 66, pp. 876-877.

38   Cf. POPE JOHN PAUL II, Encyclical Letter, *Ecclesia de Eucharistia*, no. 52: AAS 95 (2003) p. 468.

39   Cf. SECOND VATICAN ECUMENICAL COUNCIL, Decree on the Pastoral Office of Bishops, *Christus Dominus*, 28 October 1965, no. 15; cf. also Constitution on the Sacred Liturgy, *Sacrosanctum Concilium*, no. 41; *Code of Canon Law*, can. 387.

40   Prayer for the Consecration of a Bishop in the Byzantine Rite, *Euchologion to mega*, Rome, 1873, p. 139.

41   Cf. ST. IGNATIUS OF ANTIOCH, *Ad Smyrn.* 8, 1: ed. F. X. Funk, I, p. 282.

42   SECOND VATICAN ECUMENICAL COUNCIL, Dogmatic Constitution on the Church, *Lumen gentium*, no. 26; cf. S. CONGREGATION OF RITES, Instruction, *Eucharisticum mysterium*, no. 7: AAS 59 (1967) p. 545; cf. also POPE JOHN PAUL II, Apostolic Exhortation, *Pastores gregis*, 16 October 2003, nos. 32-41: *L'Osservatore Romano*, 17 October 2003, pp. 6-8.

20. Indeed, the pre-eminent manifestation of the Church is found whenever the Rites of Mass are celebrated, especially in the cathedral church, "with the full and active participation of the entire holy People of God, joined in one act of prayer, at one altar at which the Bishop presides," surrounded by his presbyterate with the Deacons and ministers.[43] Furthermore, "every lawful celebration of the Eucharist is directed by the Bishop, to whom is entrusted the office of presenting the worship of the Christian religion to the Divine Majesty and ordering it according to the precepts of the Lord and the laws of the Church, further specified by his own particular judgment for the Diocese."[44]

21. It pertains to the diocesan Bishop, then, "within the limits of his competence, to set forth liturgical norms in his Diocese, by which all are bound."[45] Still, the Bishop must take care not to allow the removal of that liberty foreseen by the norms of the liturgical books so that the celebration may be adapted in an intelligent manner to the church building, or to the group of the faithful who are present, or to particular pastoral circumstances in such a way that the universal sacred Rite is truly accommodated to human understanding.[46]

22. The Bishop governs the particular Church entrusted to him,[47] and it is his task to regulate, to direct, to encourage, and sometimes also to

---

43   Cf. SECOND VATICAN ECUMENICAL COUNCIL, Constitution on the Sacred Liturgy, *Sacrosanctum Concilium*, no. 41; cf. ST. IGNATIUS OF ANTIOCH, *Ad Magn.* 7, *Ad Philad.* 4, *Ad Smyrn.* 8: ed. F. X. Funk, I, pp. 236, 266, 281; MISSALE ROMANUM, Institutio Generalis, no. 22; cf. also *Code of Canon Law*, can. 389.

44   SECOND VATICAN ECUMENICAL COUNCIL, Constitution on the Sacred Liturgy, *Lumen gentium*, no. 26.

45   *Code of Canon Law*, can. 838 §4.

46   Cf. CONSILIUM FOR IMPLEMENTING THE CONSTITUTION ON THE LITURGY, Dubium: *Notitiae* 1 (1965) p. 254.

47   Cf. Acts 20:28; SECOND VATICAN ECUMENICAL COUNCIL, Dogmatic Constitution on the Church, *Lumen gentium*, nos. 21, 27; Decree on the Pastoral Office of Bishops in the Church, *Christus Dominus*, no. 3.

reprove;[48] this is a sacred task that he has received through episcopal Ordination,[49] which he fulfills in order to build up his flock in truth and holiness.[50] He should elucidate the inherent meaning of the Rites and the liturgical texts, and nourish the spirit of the Liturgy in the Priests, Deacons and lay faithful[51] so that they are all led to the active and fruitful celebration of the Eucharist,[52] and in like manner he should take care to ensure that the whole body of the Church is able to grow in the same understanding, in the unity of charity, in the diocese, in the nation and in the world.[53]

23. The faithful "should cling to the Bishop as the Church does to Jesus Christ, and as Jesus Christ does to the Father, so that all may be in harmonious unity, and that they may abound to the glory of God."[54] All, including members of Institutes of consecrated life and Societies of apostolic life as well as those of all ecclesial associations and movements of any kind, are subject to the authority of the diocesan Bishop in all liturgical matters,[55] apart from rights that have been legitimately conceded. To the diocesan Bishop therefore falls the right and duty of overseeing and attending to churches and oratories in his territory in

---

48   Cf. S. CONGREGATION FOR DIVINE WORSHIP, Instruction, *Liturgicae instaurationes*, 5 September 1970: AAS 62 (1970) p. 694.

49   Cf. SECOND VATICAN ECUMENICAL COUNCIL, Dogmatic Constitution on the Church, *Lumen gentium*, no. 21; Decree on the Pastoral Office of Bishops in the Church, *Christus Dominus*, no. 3.

50   Cf. CAEREMONIALE EPISCOPORUM, ex decreto sacrosancti Oecumenici Concilii Vaticani II instauratum, auctoritate Ioannis Pauli Pp. II promulgatum, editio typica, 14 September 1984, Vatican Polyglot Press, 1985, no. 10.

51   Cf. MISSALE ROMANUM, Institutio Generalis, no. 387.

52   Cf. ibid., no. 22.

53   Cf. S. CONGREGATION FOR DIVINE WORSHIP, Instruction, *Liturgicae instaurationes*: AAS 62 (1970) p. 694.

54   SECOND VATICAN ECUMENICAL COUNCIL, Dogmatic Constitution on the Church, *Lumen gentium*, no. 27; cf. 2 Cor 4:15.

55   Cf. *Code of Canon Law*, cann. 397 §1, 678 §1.

regard to liturgical matters, and this is true also of those which are founded by members of the above-mentioned institutes or under their direction, provided that the faithful are accustomed to frequent them.[56]

24. It is the right of the Christian people themselves that their diocesan Bishop should take care to prevent the occurrence of abuses in ecclesiastical discipline, especially as regards the ministry of the word, the celebration of the Sacraments and sacramentals, the worship of God and devotion to the Saints.[57]

25. Commissions as well as councils or committees established by the Bishop to handle "the promotion of the Liturgy, sacred music and art in his diocese" should act in accordance with the intentions and the norms of the Bishop; they must rely on his authority and his approval so that they may carry out their office in a suitable manner[58] and so that the effective governance of the Bishop in his diocese will be preserved. As regards all these sorts of bodies and other entities and all undertakings in liturgical matters, there has long been the need for the Bishops to consider whether their working has been fruitful thus far,[59] and to consider carefully which changes or improvements should be made in their composition and activity[60] so that they might find new vigor. It should be borne in mind that the experts are to be chosen from among those whose soundness in the Catholic faith and knowledge of theological and cultural matters are evident.

---

56   Cf. ibid., can. 683 §1.
57   Ibid., can. 392.
58   Cf. POPE JOHN PAUL II, Apostolic Letter, *Vicesimus quintus annus*, no. 21: AAS 81 (1989) p. 917; SECOND VATICAN ECUMENICAL COUNCIL, Constitution on the Sacred Liturgy, *Sacrosanctum Concilium*, nos. 45-46; POPE PIUS XII, Encyclical Letter, *Mediator Dei*: AAS 39 (1947) p. 562.
59   Cf. POPE JOHN PAUL II, Apostolic Letter, *Vicesimus quintus annus*, no. 20: AAS 81 (1989) p. 916.
60   Cf. ibid.

2. THE CONFERENCE OF BISHOPS

26. The same holds for those commissions of this kind which have been established by the Conference of Bishops in accordance with the will of the Council,[61] commissions whose members consist of Bishops who are clearly distinguished from their expert helpers. Where the number of members of a Conference of Bishops is not sufficient for the effective establishment of a liturgical commission from among their own number, then a council or group of experts should be named, always under the presidency of a Bishop, which is to fulfill the same role insofar as possible, albeit without the name of "liturgical commission."

27. As early as the year 1970, the Apostolic See announced the cessation of all experimentation as regards the celebration of Holy Mass[62] and reiterated the same in 1988.[63] Accordingly, individual Bishops and their Conferences do not have the faculty to permit experimentation with liturgical texts or the other matters that are prescribed in the liturgical books. In order to carry out experimentation of this kind in the future, the permission of the Congregation for Divine Worship and the Discipline of the Sacraments is required. It must be in writing, and it is to be requested by the Conference of Bishops. In fact, it will not be granted without serious reason As regards projects of inculturation in liturgical matters, the particular norms that have been established are strictly and comprehensively to be observed.[64]

---

61   Cf. SECOND VATICAN ECUMENICAL COUNCIL, Constitution on the Sacred Liturgy, *Sacrosanctum Concilium*, no. 44; CONGREGATION FOR BISHOPS, Letter sent to the Presidents of the Conferences of Bishops together with the Congregation for the Evangelization of Peoples, 21 June 1999, no. 9: AAS 91 (1999) p. 999.

62   Cf. CONGREGATION FOR DIVINE WORSHIP, Instruction, *Liturgicae instaurationis*, no. 12: AAS 62 (1970) pp. 692-704, here p. 703.

63   Cf. CONGREGATION FOR DIVINE WORSHIP, *Declaration on Eucharistic Prayers and Liturgical Experimentation*, 21 March 1988: *Notitiae* 24 (1988) pp. 234-236.

64   Cf. CONGREGATION FOR DIVINE WORSHIP AND THE DISCIPLINE OF THE SACRAMENTS, Instruction, *Varietates legitimae*: AAS 87 (1995) pp. 288-314.

28. All liturgical norms that a Conference of Bishops will have established for its territory in accordance with the law are to be submitted to the Congregation for Divine Worship and the Discipline of the Sacraments for the *recognitio*, without which they lack any binding force.[65]

3. PRIESTS

29. Priests, as capable, prudent and indispensable co-workers of the order of Bishops,[66] called to the service of the People of God, constitute one presbyterate with their Bishop,[67] though charged with differing offices. "In each local congregation of the faithful, in a certain way, they make present the Bishop with whom they are associated in trust and in generosity of heart; according to their rank, they take upon themselves his duties and his solicitude, and they carry these out in their daily work." And "because of this participation in the Priesthood and mission, Priests should recognize the Bishop as truly their father and obey him reverently."[68] Furthermore, "ever intent upon the good of God's children, they should seek to contribute to the pastoral mission of the whole diocese, and indeed of the whole Church."[69]

---

65 Cf. *Code of Canon Law*, can. 838 §3; S. CONGREGATION OF RITES, Instruction, *Inter Oecumenici*, 26 September 1964, no. 31: AAS 56 (1964) p. 883; CONGREGATION FOR DIVINE WORSHIP AND THE DISCIPLINE OF THE SACRAMENTS, Instruction, *Liturgiam authenticam*, nos. 79-80: AAS 93 (2001) pp. 711-713.

66 Cf. SECOND VATICAN ECUMENICAL COUNCIL, Decree on the Ministry and Life of Priests, *Presbyterorum ordinis*, 7 December 1965, no. 7; PONTIFICALE ROMANUM, ed. 1962: Ordo consecrationis sacerdotalis, in Praefatione; PONTIFICALE ROMANUM *ex decreto sacrosancti Oecumenici Concilii Vaticani II renovatum, auctoritate Pauli Pp. VI editum, Ioannis Pauli Pp. II cura recognitum*: De Ordinatione Episcopi, presbyterorum et diaconorum, editio typica altera, 29 June 1989, Typis Polyglottis Vaticanis, 1990, Chapter II: *De Ordin. presbyterorum*, Praenotanda, no. 101.

67 ST. IGNATIUS OF ANTIOCH, *Ad Philad.* 4: ed. F. X. Funk, I, p. 266; POPE ST. CORNELIUS I, cited by St. Cyprian, Letter 48, 2: ed. G. Hartel, III, 2, p. 610.

68 SECOND VATICAN ECUMENICAL COUNCIL, Dogmatic Constitution on the Church, *Lumen gentium*, no. 28.

69 Cf. ibid.

30. The office "that belongs to Priests in particular in the celebration of the Eucharist" is a great one, "for it is their responsibility to preside at the Eucharist *in persona Christi* and to provide a witness to and a service of communion not only for the community directly taking part in the celebration, but also for the universal Church, which is always brought into play within the context of the Eucharist. It must be lamented that, especially in the years following the post-Conciliar liturgical reform, as a result of a misguided sense of creativity and adaptation, there have been a number of abuses which have been a source of suffering for many."[70]

31. In keeping with the solemn promises that they have made in the Rite of Sacred Ordination and renewed each year in the Mass of the Chrism, let Priests celebrate "devoutly and faithfully the mysteries of Christ for the praise of God and the sanctification of the Christian people, according to the tradition of the Church, especially in the Eucharistic Sacrifice and in the Sacrament of Reconciliation."[71] They ought not to detract from the profound meaning of their own ministry by corrupting the liturgical celebration either through alteration or omission, or through arbitrary additions.[72] For as St. Ambrose said, "It is not in herself . . . but in us that the Church is injured. Let us take care so that our own failure may not cause injury to the Church."[73] Let the Church of God not be

---

70   POPE JOHN PAUL II, Encyclical Letter, *Ecclesia de Eucharistia*, no. 52; cf. no. 29: AAS 95 (2003) pp. 467-468, 452-435.

71   PONTIFICALE ROMANUM, De Ordinatione Episcopi, presbyterorum et diaconorum, editio typica altera: *De Ordinatione Presbyterorum*, no. 124; cf. MISSALE ROMANUM, Feria V in Hebdomada Sancta: Ad Missam chrismatis, Renovatio promissionum sacerdotalium, p. 292.

72   Cf. ECUMENICAL COUNCIL OF TRENT, Session VII, 3 March 1547, Decree on the Sacraments, can. 13, DS 1613; SECOND VATICAN ECUMENICAL COUNCIL, Constitution on the Sacred Liturgy, *Sacrosanctum Concilium*, no. 22; POPE PIUS XII, Encyclical Letter, *Mediator Dei*: AAS 39 (1947) pp. 544, 546-547, 562; *Code of Canon Law*, can. 846, §1; MISSALE ROMANUM, Institutio Generalis, no. 24.

73   ST. AMBROSE, *De Virginitate*, no. 48: PL 16, 278.

injured, then, by Priests who have so solemnly dedicated themselves to the ministry. Indeed, under the Bishop's authority let them faithfully seek to prevent others as well from committing this type of distortion.

32. "Let the Parish Priest strive so that the Most Holy Eucharist will be the center of the parish congregation of the faithful; let him work to ensure that Christ's faithful are nourished through the devout celebration of the Sacraments, and in particular, that they frequently approach the Most Holy Eucharist and the Sacrament of Penance; let him strive, furthermore, to ensure that the faithful are encouraged to offer prayers in their families as well, and to participate consciously and actively in the Sacred Liturgy, which the Parish Priest, under the authority of the diocesan Bishop, is bound to regulate and supervise in his parish lest abuses occur."[74] Although it is appropriate that he should be assisted in the effective preparation of the liturgical celebrations by various members of Christ's faithful, he nevertheless must not cede to them in any way those things that are proper to his own office.

33. Finally, all "Priests should go to the trouble of properly cultivating their liturgical knowledge and ability, so that through their liturgical ministry, God the Father, Son and Holy Spirit will be praised in an ever more excellent manner by the Christian communities entrusted to them."[75] Above all, let them be filled with that wonder and amazement that the Paschal Mystery, in being celebrated, instills in the hearts of the faithful.[76]

---

74 *Code of Canon Law*, can. 528 §2.
75 SECOND VATICAN ECUMENICAL COUNCIL, Decree on the Ministry and Life of Priests, *Presbyterorum Ordinis*, no. 5.
76 Cf. POPE JOHN PAUL II, Encyclical Letter, *Ecclesia de Eucharistia*, no. 5: AAS 95 (2003) p. 436.

4. DEACONS

34. Deacons "upon whom hands are imposed not for the Priesthood but for the ministry,"[77] as men of good repute,[78] must act in such a way that with the help of God they may be recognized as the true disciples[79] of him "who came not to be served but to serve,"[80] and who was among his disciples "as one who serves."[81] Strengthened by the gift of the Holy Spirit through the laying on of hands, they are in service to the People of God, in communion with the Bishop and his presbyterate.[82] They should therefore consider the Bishop as a father, and give assistance to him and to the Priests "in the ministry of the word, of the altar, and of charity."[83]

35. Let them never fail, "as the Apostle says, to hold the mystery of faith with a clear conscience,[84] and to proclaim this faith by word and deed according to the Gospel and the tradition of the Church,"[85] in wholehearted, faithful and humble service to the Sacred Liturgy as the source and summit of ecclesial life, "so that all, made children of God through faith and Baptism, may come together as one, praising God in the midst of the Church, to participate in the Sacrifice and to eat the Lord's Supper."[86] Let all Deacons, then, do their part so that the Sacred Liturgy will be celebrated according to the norms of the duly approved liturgical books.

---

77   SECOND VATICAN ECUMENICAL COUNCIL, Dogmatic Constitution on the Church, *Lumen gentium*, no. 29; cf. *Constitutiones Ecclesiae Aegypticae*, III, 2: ed. F. X. Funk, *Didascalia*, II, p. 103; *Statuta Ecclesiae Ant.*, 37-41: ed. D. Mansi 3, 954.

78   Cf. Acts 6:3.

79   Jn 13:35.

80   Mt 20:28.

81   Cf. Lk 22:27.

82   Cf. CAEREMONIALE EPISCOPORUM, nos. 9, 23. Cf. SECOND VATICAN ECUMENICAL COUNCIL, Dogmatic Constitution on the Church, *Lumen gentium*, no. 29.

83   Cf. PONTIFICALE ROMANUM, De Ordinatione Episcopi, presbyterorum et diaconorum, editio typica altera, Chapter III, *De Ordin. diaconorum*, no. 199.

84   Cf. 1 Tim 3:9.

85   Cf. PONTIFICALE ROMANUM, De Ordinatione Episcopi, presbyterorum et diaconorum, editio typica altera, Chapter III, *De Ordin. diaconorum*, no. 200.

86   SECOND VATICAN ECUMENICAL COUNCIL, Constitution on the Sacred Liturgy, *Sacrosanctum Concilium*, no. 10.

CHAPTER II
The Participation of the Lay Christian Faithful in the Eucharistic Celebration

1. ACTIVE AND CONSCIOUS PARTICIPATION

36. The celebration of the Mass, as the action of Christ and of the Church, is the center of the whole Christian life for the universal as well as the particular Church, and also for the individual faithful,[87] who are involved "in differing ways according to the diversity of orders, ministries, and active participation."[88] In this way the Christian people, "a chosen race, a royal priesthood, a holy people, a people God has made his own,"[89] manifests its coherent and hierarchical ordering."[90] "For the common priesthood of the faithful and the ministerial or hierarchical Priesthood, though they differ in essence and not only in degree, are ordered to one another, for both partake, each in its own way, of the one Priesthood of Christ."[91]

---

87   Cf. ibid., no. 41; SECOND VATICAN ECUMENICAL COUNCIL, Dogmatic Constitution on the Church, *Lumen gentium*, no. 11; Decree on the Ministry and Life of Priests, *Presbyterorum ordinis*, nos. 2, 5, 6; Decree on the Pastoral Office of Bishops, *Christus Dominus*, no. 30; Decree on Ecumenism, *Unitatis redintegratio*, 21 November 1964, no. 15; S. CONGREGATION OF RITES, Instruction, *Eucharisticum mysterium*, nos. 3e, 6: AAS 59 (1967) pp. 542, 544-545; MISSALE ROMANUM, Institutio Generalis, no. 16.

88   Cf. SECOND VATICAN ECUMENICAL COUNCIL, Constitution on the Sacred Liturgy, *Sacrosanctum Concilium*, no. 26; MISSALE ROMANUM, Institutio Generalis, no. 91.

89   1 Pt 2:9; cf. nos. 2, 4-5.

90   MISSALE ROMANUM, Institutio Generalis, no. 91; cf. SECOND VATICAN ECUMENICAL COUNCIL, Constitution on the Sacred Liturgy, *Sacrosanctum Concilium*, no. 41.

91   SECOND VATICAN ECUMENICAL COUNCIL, Dogmatic Constitution on the Church, *Lumen gentium*, no. 10.

37. All of Christ's faithful, freed from their sins and incorporated into the Church through Baptism, are deputed by means of a sacramental character for the worship of the Christian religion,[92] so that by virtue of their royal priesthood,[93] persevering in prayer and praising God,[94] they may offer themselves as a living and holy sacrifice pleasing to God and attested to others by their works,[95] giving witness to Christ throughout the earth and providing an answer to those who ask concerning their hope of eternal life that is in them.[96] Thus the participation of the lay faithful too in the Eucharist and in the other celebrations of the Church's Rites cannot be equated with mere presence, and still less with a passive one, but is rather to be regarded as a true exercise of faith and of the baptismal dignity.

38. The constant teaching of the Church on the nature of the Eucharist not only as a meal, but also and pre-eminently as a Sacrifice, is therefore rightly understood to be one of the principal keys to the full participation of all the faithful in so great a Sacrament.[97] For when "stripped of its sacrificial meaning, the mystery is understood as if its meaning and importance were simply that of a fraternal banquet."[98]

39. For promoting and elucidating active participation, the recent renewal of the liturgical books according to the mind of the Council fostered acclamations of the people, responses, psalmody, antiphons, and canticles, as well as actions or movements and gestures, and called for

---

92   Cf. St. Thomas Aquinas, *Summa Theol.*, III, q. 63, a. 2.
93   Second Vatican Ecumenical Council, Dogmatic Constitution on the Church, *Lumen gentium*, no. 10; cf. Pope John Paul II, Encyclical Letter, *Ecclesia de Eucharistia*, no. 28: AAS 95 (2003) p. 452.
94   Cf. Acts 2:42-47.
95   Cf. Rom 12:1.
96   Cf. 1 Pt 3:15, 2:4-10.
97   Cf. Pope John Paul II, Encyclical Letter, *Ecclesia de Eucharistia*, nos. 12-18: AAS 95 (2003) p. 441-445; Letter, *Dominicae Cenae*, 24 February 1980, no. 9: AAS 72 (1980) pp. 129-133.
98   Pope John Paul II, Encyclical Letter, *Ecclesia de Eucharistia*, no. 10: AAS 95 (2003) p. 439.

sacred silence to be maintained at the proper times, while providing rubrics for the parts of the faithful as well.[99] In addition, ample flexibility is given for appropriate creativity aimed at allowing each celebration to be adapted to the needs of the participants, to their comprehension, their interior preparation and their gifts, according to the established liturgical norms. In the songs, the melodies, the choice of prayers and readings, the giving of the homily, the preparation of the prayer of the faithful, the occasional explanatory remarks, and the decoration of the church building according to the various seasons, there is ample possibility for introducing into each celebration a certain variety by which the riches of the liturgical tradition will also be more clearly evident, and so, in keeping with pastoral requirements, the celebration will be carefully imbued with those particular features that will foster the recollection of the participants. Still, it should be remembered that the power of the liturgical celebrations does not consist in frequently altering the Rites, but in probing more deeply the word of God and the mystery being celebrated.[100]

40. Nevertheless, from the fact that the liturgical celebration obviously entails activity, it does not follow that everyone must necessarily have something concrete to do beyond the actions and gestures, as if a certain specific liturgical ministry must necessarily be given to the individuals to be carried out by them. Instead, catechetical instruction should strive diligently to correct those widespread superficial notions and practices often seen in recent years in this regard, and ever to instill anew in all of Christ's faithful that sense of deep wonder before the greatness of the mystery of faith that is the Eucharist, in whose celebration the Church is forever passing from what is obsolete into newness of life: *"in novitatem a vetustate."*[101] For in the celebration of the

---

99   Cf. Second Vatican Ecumenical Council, Constitution on the Sacred Liturgy, *Sacrosanctum Concilium*, nos. 30-31.

100 Cf. S. Congregation for Divine Worship, Instruction, *Liturgicae instaurationes*, no. 1: AAS 62 (1970) p. 695.

101 Cf. Missale Romanum, Feria secunda post Dominica V in Quadragesima, Collecta, p. 258.

Eucharist, as in the whole Christian life which draws its power from it and leads toward it, the Church, after the manner of St. Thomas the Apostle, prostrates herself in adoration before the Lord who was crucified, suffered and died, was buried and arose, and perpetually exclaims to him who is clothed in the fullness of his divine splendor: "My Lord and my God!"[102]

41. For encouraging, promoting and nourishing this interior understanding of liturgical participation, the continuous and widespread celebration of the Liturgy of the Hours, the use of the sacramentals and exercises of Christian popular piety are extremely helpful. These latter exercises—which "while not belonging to the Liturgy in the strict sense, possess nonetheless a particular importance and dignity"—are to be regarded as having a certain connection with the liturgical context, especially when they have been lauded and attested by the Magisterium itself,[103] as is the case especially of the Marian Rosary.[104] Furthermore, since these practices of piety lead the Christian people both to the reception of the Sacraments—especially the Eucharist—and "to meditation on the mysteries of our Redemption and the imitation of the excellent heavenly examples of the Saints, they are therefore not without salutary effects for our participation in liturgical worship."[105]

42. It must be acknowledged that the Church has not come together by human volition; rather, she has been called together by God in the Holy

---

102   Cf. POPE JOHN PAUL II, Apostolic Letter, *Novo Millennio ineunte*, 6 January 2001, no. 21: AAS 93 (2001) p. 280; cf. Jn 20:28.
103   Cf. POPE PIUS XII, Encyclical Letter, *Mediator Dei*: AAS 39 (1947) p. 586; cf. also SECOND VATICAN ECUMENICAL COUNCIL, Dogmatic Constitution on the Church, *Lumen gentium*, no. 67; POPE PAUL VI, Apostolic Exhortation, *Marialis cultus*, 11 February 1974, no. 24: AAS 66 (1974) pp. 113-168, here p. 134; CONGREGATION FOR DIVINE WORSHIP AND THE DISCIPLINE OF THE SACRAMENTS, *Direttorio su pieta popolare e Liturgia*, 17 December 2001.
104   POPE JOHN PAUL II, Apostolic Letter, *Rosarium Virginis Mariae*, 16 October 2002: AAS 95 (2003) pp. 5-36.
105   Cf. POPE PIUS XII, Encyclical Letter, *Mediator Dei*: AAS 39 (1947) pp. 586-587.

Spirit, and she responds through faith to his free calling (thus the word *"ekklesia"* is related to *"klesis,"* or "calling").[106] Nor is the Eucharistic Sacrifice to be considered a "concelebration," in the univocal sense, of the Priest along with the people who are present.[107] On the contrary, the Eucharist celebrated by the Priests "is a gift which radically transcends the power of the community. . . . The community that gathers for the celebration of the Eucharist absolutely requires an ordained Priest, who presides over it so that it may truly be a eucharistic convocation. On the other hand, the community is by itself incapable of providing an ordained minister."[108] There is pressing need of a concerted will to avoid all ambiguity in this matter and to remedy the difficulties of recent years. Accordingly, terms such as "celebrating community" or "celebrating assembly" (in other languages *"asamblea celebrante,"* *"assemblée célébrante,"* *"assemblea celebrante"*) and similar terms should not be used injudiciously.

2. THE MINISTRIES OF THE LAY CHRISTIAN FAITHFUL IN THE CELEBRATION OF HOLY MASS

43. For the good of the community and of the whole Church of God, some of the lay faithful according to tradition have rightly and laudably exercised ministries in the celebration of the Sacred Liturgy.[109] It is appropriate that a number of persons distribute among themselves and exercise various ministries or different parts of the same ministry.[110]

---

106 Cf. CONGREGATION FOR DIVINE WORSHIP AND THE DISCIPLINE OF THE SACRAMENTS, Instruction, *Varietates legitimae,* no. 22: AAS 87 (1995) p. 297.

107 Cf. POPE PIUS XII, Encyclical Letter, *Mediator Dei:* AAS 39 (1947) p. 553.

108 POPE JOHN PAUL II, Encyclical Letter, *Ecclesia de Eucharistia,* no. 29: AAS 95 (2003) p. 453; cf. FOURTH LATERAN ECUMENICAL COUNCIL, 11-30 November 1215, Chapter I: DS 802; ECUMENICAL COUNCIL OF TRENT, Session XXIII, 15 July 1563, *Doctrine and Canons on Sacred Order,* Chapter 4: DS 1767-1770; POPE PIUS XII, Encyclical Letter, *Mediator Dei:* AAS 39 (1947) p. 553.

109 Cf. *Code of Canon Law,* can. 230 §2; cf. also MISSALE ROMANUM, Institutio Generalis, no. 97.

110 Cf. MISSALE ROMANUM, Institutio Generalis, no. 109.

44. Apart from the duly instituted ministries of acolyte and lector,[111] the most important of these ministries are those of acolyte[112] and lector[113] by temporary deputation. In addition to these are the other functions that are described in the Roman Missal,[114] as well as the functions of preparing the hosts, washing the liturgical linens, and the like. All, "whether ordained ministers or lay faithful, in exercising their own office or ministry should do exclusively and fully that which pertains to them."[115] In the liturgical celebration itself as well as in its preparation, they should do what is necessary so that the Church's Liturgy will be carried out worthily and appropriately.

45. To be avoided is the danger of obscuring the complementary relationship between the action of clerics and that of laypersons, in such a way that the ministry of laypersons undergoes what might be called a

---

111 Cf. POPE PAUL VI, Apostolic Letter (Motu Proprio), MINISTERIA QUAEDAM, 15 August 1972, nos. 6-12; PONTIFICALE ROMANUM *ex decreto sacrosancti oecumenici Concilii Vaticani II instauratum, auctoritate Pauli Pp. VI promulgatum,* De institutione lectorum et acolythorum, de admissione inter candidatos ad diaconatum et presbyteratum, de sacro caelibatu amplectendo, editio typica, 3 December 1972, Typis Polyglottis Vaticanis, 1973, p. 10: AAS 64 (1972) pp. 529-534, here pp. 532-533; *Code of Canon Law,* can. 230 §1; MISSALE ROMANUM, Institutio Generalis, nos. 98-99, 187-193.

112 Cf. MISSALE ROMANUM, Institutio Generalis, nos. 187-190, 193; *Code of Canon Law,* can. 230 §2-3.

113 Cf. SECOND VATICAN ECUMENICAL COUNCIL, Constitution on the Sacred Liturgy, *Sacrosanctum Concilium,* no. 24; S. CONGREGATION FOR THE SACRAMENTS AND DIVINE WORSHIP, Instruction, *Inaestimabile donum,* nos. 2, 18: AAS 72 (1980) pp. 334, 338; MISSALE ROMANUM, Institutio Generalis, nos. 101, 194-198; *Code of Canon Law,* can. 230 §2-3.

114 Cf. MISSALE ROMANUM, Institutio Generalis, nos. 100-107.

115 Ibid., no. 91; cf. SECOND VATICAN ECUMENICAL COUNCIL, Constitution on the Sacred Liturgy, *Sacrosanctum Concilium,* no. 28.

certain "clericalization," while the sacred ministers inappropriately assume those things that are proper to the life and activity of the lay faithful.[116]

46. The lay Christian faithful called to give assistance at liturgical celebrations should be well instructed and must be those whose Christian life, morals and fidelity to the Church's Magisterium recommend them. It is fitting that such a one should have received a liturgical formation in accordance with his or her age, condition, state of life, and religious culture.[117] No one should be selected whose designation could cause consternation for the faithful.[118]

47. It is altogether laudable to maintain the noble custom by which boys or youths, customarily termed "servers," provide service of the altar after the manner of acolytes, and receive catechesis regarding their function in accordance with their power of comprehension.[119] Nor should it be forgotten that a great number of sacred ministers over the course of the centuries have come from among boys such as these.[120] Associations

---

116 Cf. POPE JOHN PAUL II, Allocution to the Conference of Bishops of the Antilles, 7 May 2002, no. 2: AAS 94 (2002) pp. 575-577; Post-Synodal Apostolic Exhortation, *Christifideles laici*, 30 December 1988, no. 23: AAS 81 (1989) pp. 393-521, here pp. 429-431; CONGREGATION FOR THE CLERGY ET AL., Instruction, *Ecclesiae de mysterio*, 15 August 1997, Theological Principles, no. 4: AAS 89 (1997) pp. 860-861.

117 Cf. SECOND VATICAN ECUMENICAL COUNCIL, Constitution on the Sacred Liturgy, *Sacrosanctum Concilium*, no. 19.

118 S. CONGREGATION FOR DIVINE WORSHIP, Instruction, *Immensae caritatis*, 29 January 1973: AAS 65 (1973) p. 266.

119 Cf. S. CONGREGATION OF RITES, Instruction, *De Musica sacra*, 3 September 1958, no. 93c: AAS 50 (1958) p. 656.

120 Cf. PONTIFICAL COUNCIL FOR THE INTERPRETATION OF LEGISLATIVE TEXTS, Response to dubium, 11 July 1992: AAS 86 (1994) pp. 541-542; CONGREGATION FOR DIVINE WORSHIP AND THE DISCIPLINE OF THE SACRAMENTS, Letter to the Presidents of Conferences of Bishops on the liturgical service of laypersons, 15 March 1994: *Notitiae* 30 (1994) pp. 333-335, 347-348.

for them, including also the participation and assistance of their parents, should be established or promoted, and in such a way greater pastoral care will be provided for the ministers. Whenever such associations are international in nature, it pertains to the competence of the Congregation for Divine Worship and the Discipline of the Sacraments to establish them or to approve and revise their statutes.[121] Girls or women may also be admitted to this service of the altar, at the discretion of the diocesan Bishop and in observance of the established norms.[122]

---

121   Cf. POPE JOHN PAUL II, Apostolic Constitution, *Pastor Bonus*, article 65: AAS 80 (1988) p. 877.

122   Cf. PONTIFICAL COUNCIL FOR THE INTERPRETATION OF LEGISLATIVE TEXTS, Response to dubium, 11 July 1992: AAS 86 (1994) pp. 541-542; CONGREGATION FOR DIVINE WORSHIP AND THE DISCIPLINE OF THE SACRAMENTS, Letter to the Presidents of the Conferences of Bishops concerning the liturgical service of laypersons, 15 March 1994: *Notitiae* 30 (1994) pp. 333-335, 347-348; Letter to a Bishop, 27 July 2001: *Notitiae* 38 (2002) 46-54.

CHAPTER III
The Proper Celebration of Mass

1. THE MATTER OF THE MOST HOLY EUCHARIST

48. The bread used in the celebration of the Most Holy Eucharistic Sacrifice must be unleavened, purely of wheat, and recently made so that there is no danger of decomposition.[123] It follows therefore that bread made from another substance, even if it is grain, or if it is mixed with another substance different from wheat to such an extent that it would not commonly be considered wheat bread, does not constitute valid matter for confecting the Sacrifice and the Eucharistic Sacrament.[124] It is a grave abuse to introduce other substances, such as fruit or sugar or honey, into the bread for confecting the Eucharist. Hosts should obviously be made by those who are not only distinguished by their integrity, but also skilled in making them and furnished with suitable tools.[125]

49. By reason of the sign, it is appropriate that at least some parts of the Eucharistic Bread coming from the fraction should be distributed to at least some of the faithful in Communion. "Small hosts are, however, in no way ruled out when the number of those receiving Holy Communion or other pastoral needs require it,"[126] and indeed small hosts requiring no further fraction ought customarily to be used for the most part.

---

123   Cf. *Code of Canon Law*, can. 924 §2; MISSALE ROMANUM, Institutio Generalis, no. 320.
124   Cf. S. CONGREGATION FOR THE DISCIPLINE OF THE SACRAMENTS, Instruction, *Dominus Salvator noster*, 26 March 1929, no. 1: AAS 21 (1929) pp. 631-642, here p. 632.
125   Cf. ibid., no. 2: AAS 21 (1929) p. 635.
126   Cf. MISSALE ROMANUM, Institutio Generalis, no. 321.

50. The wine that is used in the most sacred celebration of the Eucharistic Sacrifice must be natural, from the fruit of the grape, pure and incorrupt, not mixed with other substances.[127] During the celebration itself, a small quantity of water is to be mixed with it. Great care should be taken so that the wine intended for the celebration of the Eucharist is well conserved and has not soured.[128] It is altogether forbidden to use wine of doubtful authenticity or provenance, for the Church requires certainty regarding the conditions necessary for the validity of the Sacraments. Nor are other drinks of any kind to be admitted for any reason, as they do not constitute valid matter.

2. THE EUCHARISTIC PRAYER

51. Only those Eucharistic Prayers are to be used which are found in the Roman Missal or are legitimately approved by the Apostolic See, and according to the manner and the terms set forth by it. "It is not to be tolerated that some Priests take upon themselves the right to compose their own Eucharistic Prayers"[129] or to change the same texts approved by the Church, or to introduce others composed by private individuals.[130]

52. The proclamation of the Eucharistic Prayer, which by its very nature is the climax of the whole celebration, is proper to the Priest by virtue of his Ordination. It is therefore an abuse to proffer it in such a way that some parts of the Eucharistic Prayer are recited by a Deacon, a lay minister, or by an individual member of the faithful, or by all

---

127   Cf. Lk 22:18; *Code of Canon Law*, can. 924 §§1, 3; MISSALE ROMANUM, Institutio Generalis, no. 322.

128   Cf. MISSALE ROMANUM, Institutio Generalis, no. 323.

129   POPE JOHN PAUL II, Apostolic Letter, *Vicesimus quintus annus*, no. 13, AAS 81 (1989).

130   S. CONGREGATION FOR THE SACRAMENTS AND DIVINE WORSHIP, Instruction, *Inaestimabile donum*, no. 5: AAS 72 (1980) p. 335.

members of the faithful together. The Eucharistic Prayer, then, is to be recited by the Priest alone in full.[131]

53. While the Priest proclaims the Eucharistic Prayer "there should be no other prayers or singing, and the organ or other musical instruments should be silent,"[132] except for the people's acclamations that have been duly approved, as described below.

54. The people, however, are always involved actively and never merely passively: for they "silently join themselves with the Priest in faith, as well as in their interventions during the course of the Eucharistic Prayer as prescribed, namely in the responses in the Preface dialogue, the *Sanctus*, the acclamation after the consecration and the '*Amen*' after the final doxology, and in other acclamations approved by the Conference of Bishops with the *recognitio* of the Holy See."[133]

55. In some places there has existed an abuse by which the Priest breaks the host at the time of the consecration in the Holy Mass. This abuse is contrary to the tradition of the Church. It is reprobated and is to be corrected with haste.

56. The mention of the name of the Supreme Pontiff and the diocesan Bishop in the Eucharistic Prayer is not to be omitted, since this is a most ancient tradition to be maintained, and a manifestation of ecclesial communion. For "the coming together of the eucharistic community is at

---

131 Cf. POPE JOHN PAUL II, Encyclical Letter, *Ecclesia de Eucharistia*, no. 28: AAS 95 (2003) p. 452; MISSALE ROMANUM, Institutio Generalis, no. 147; S. CONGREGATION FOR DIVINE WORSHIP, Instruction, *Liturgicae instaurationes*, no. 4: AAS 62 (1970) p. 698; S. CONGREGATION FOR THE SACRAMENTS AND DIVINE WORSHIP, Instruction, *Inaestimabile donum*, no. 4: AAS 72 (1980) p. 334.

132 MISSALE ROMANUM, Institutio Generalis, no. 32.

133 Ibid., no. 147; cf. POPE JOHN PAUL II, Encyclical Letter, *Ecclesia de Eucharistia*, no. 28: AAS 95 (2003) p. 452; cf. also CONGREGATION FOR THE SACRAMENTS AND DIVINE WORSHIP, Instruction, *Inaestimabile donum*, no. 4: AAS 72 (1980) pp. 334-335.

the same time a joining in union with its own Bishop and with the Roman Pontiff."[134]

3. THE OTHER PARTS OF THE MASS

57. It is the right of the community of Christ's faithful that especially in the Sunday celebration there should customarily be true and suitable sacred music, and that there should always be an altar, vestments and sacred linens that are dignified, proper, and clean, in accordance with the norms.

58. All of Christ's faithful likewise have the right to a celebration of the Eucharist that has been so carefully prepared in all its parts that the word of God is properly and efficaciously proclaimed and explained in it; that the faculty for selecting the liturgical texts and Rites is carried out with care according to the norms; and that their faith is duly safeguarded and nourished by the words that are sung in the celebration of the Liturgy.

59. The reprobated practice by which Priests, Deacons or the faithful here and there alter or vary at will the texts of the Sacred Liturgy that they are charged to pronounce, must cease. For in doing thus, they render the celebration of the Sacred Liturgy unstable, and not infrequently distort the authentic meaning of the Liturgy.

60. In the celebration of Mass, the Liturgy of the Word and the Liturgy of the Eucharist are intimately connected to one another, and form one single act of worship. For this reason it is not licit to separate one of these parts from the other and celebrate them at different times or places.[135] Nor is it licit to carry out the individual parts of Holy Mass at different times of the same day.

---

134   POPE JOHN PAUL II, Encyclical Letter, *Ecclesia de Eucharistia*, no. 39: AAS 95 (2003) p. 459.

135   Cf. S. CONGREGATION FOR DIVINE WORSHIP, Instruction, *Liturgicae instaurationes*, no. 2b: AAS 62 (1970) p. 696.

61. In selecting the biblical readings for proclamation in the celebration of Mass, the norms found in the liturgical books are to be followed,[136] so that indeed "a richer table of the word of God will be prepared for the faithful, and the biblical treasures opened up for them."[137]

62. It is also illicit to omit or to substitute the prescribed biblical readings on one's own initiative, and especially "to substitute other, non-biblical texts for the readings and responsorial Psalm, which contain the word of God."[138]

63. "Within the celebration of the Sacred Liturgy, the reading of the Gospel, which is "the high point of the Liturgy of the Word,"[139] is reserved by the Church's tradition to an ordained minister.[140] Thus it is not permitted for a layperson, even a religious, to proclaim the Gospel reading in the celebration of Holy Mass, nor in other cases in which the norms do not explicitly permit it.[141]

64. The homily, which is given in the course of the celebration of Holy Mass and is a part of the Liturgy itself,[142] "should ordinarily be given

---

136   Cf. MISSALE ROMANUM, Institutio Generalis, nos. 356-362.

137   Cf. SECOND VATICAN ECUMENICAL COUNCIL, Constitution on the Sacred Liturgy, *Sacrosanctum Concilium*, no. 51.

138   MISSALE ROMANUM, Institutio Generalis, no. 57; cf. POPE JOHN PAUL II, Apostolic Letter, *Vicesimus quintus annus*, no. 13: AAS 81 (1989) p. 910; CONGREGATION FOR THE DOCTRINE OF THE FAITH, Declaration, *Dominus Iesus*, on the unicity and salvific universality of Jesus Christ and the Church, 6 August 2000: AAS 92 (2000) pp. 742-765.

139   MISSALE ROMANUM, Institutio Generalis, no. 60.

140   Cf. ibid., nos. 59-60.

141   Cf., e.g., RITUALE ROMANUM, *ex decreto sacrosancti Oecumenici Concilii Vaticani II renovatum, auctoritate Pauli Pp. VI editum Ioannis Pauli Pp. II cura recognitum*: Ordo celebrandi Matrimonium, editio typica altera, 19 March 1990, Typis Polyglottis Vaticanis 1991, no. 125; ROMAN RITUAL, renewed by decree of the Second Vatican Ecumenical Council and promulgated by authority of Pope Paul VI: Order for Anointing of the Sick and for their Pastoral Care, editio typica, 7 December 1972, Vatican Polyglot Press, 1972, no. 72.

142   Cf. *Code of Canon Law*, can. 767 §1.

by the Priest celebrant himself. He may entrust it to a concelebrating Priest or occasionally, according to circumstances, to a Deacon, but never to a layperson.[143] In particular cases and for a just cause, the homily may even be given by a Bishop or a Priest who is present at the celebration but cannot concelebrate."[144]

65. It should be borne in mind that any previous norm that may have admitted non-ordained faithful to give the homily during the eucharistic celebration is to be considered abrogated by the norm of canon 767 §1.[145] This practice is reprobated, so that it cannot be permitted to attain the force of custom.

66. The prohibition of the admission of laypersons to preach within the Mass applies also to seminarians, students of theological disciplines, and those who have assumed the function of those known as "pastoral assistants"; nor is there to be any exception for any other kind of layperson, or group, or community, or association.[146]

67. Particular care is to be taken so that the homily is firmly based upon the mysteries of salvation, expounding the mysteries of the Faith and the norms of Christian life from the biblical readings and liturgical texts throughout the course of the liturgical year and providing commentary on the texts of the Ordinary or the Proper of the Mass, or

---

143   Cf. MISSALE ROMANUM, Institutio Generalis, no. 66; cf. also *Code of Canon Law*, can. 6, §§1, 2; also can. 767 §1, regarding which other noteworthy prescriptions may be found in CONGREGATION FOR THE CLERGY ET AL., Instruction, *Ecclesiae de mysterio*, Practical Provisions, article 3 §1: AAS 89 (1997) p. 865.

144   MISSALE ROMANUM, Institutio Generalis, no. 66; cf. also *Code of Canon Law*, can. 767 §1.

145   Cf. CONGREGATION FOR THE CLERGY ET AL., Instruction, *Ecclesiae de mysterio*, Practical Provisions, article 3 §1: AAS 89 (1997) p. 865; cf. also *Code of Canon Law*, can. 6 §§1, 2; PONTIFICAL COMMISSION FOR THE AUTHENTIC INTERPRETATION OF THE CODE OF CANON LAW, Response to dubium, 20 June 1987: AAS 79 (1987) p. 1249.

146   Cf. CONGREGATION FOR THE CLERGY ET AL., Instruction, *Ecclesiae de mysterio*, Practical Provisions, article 3 §1: AAS 89 (1997) pp. 864-865.

of some other Rite of the Church.[147] It is clear that all interpretations of Sacred Scripture are to be referred back to Christ himself as the one upon whom the entire economy of salvation hinges, though this should be done in light of the specific context of the liturgical celebration. In the homily to be given, care is to be taken so that the light of Christ may shine upon life's events. Even so, this is to be done so as not to obscure the true and unadulterated word of God: for instance, treating only of politics or profane subjects, or drawing upon notions derived from contemporary pseudo-religious currents as a source.[148]

68. The diocesan Bishop must diligently oversee the preaching of the homily,[149] also publishing norms and distributing guidelines and auxiliary tools to the sacred ministers, and promoting meetings and other projects for this purpose so that they may have the opportunity to consider the nature of the homily more precisely and find help in its preparation.

69. In Holy Mass as well as in other celebrations of the Sacred Liturgy, no Creed or Profession of Faith is to be introduced which is not found in the duly approved liturgical books.

70. The offerings that Christ's faithful are accustomed to present for the Liturgy of the Eucharist in Holy Mass are not necessarily limited to bread and wine for the eucharistic celebration, but may also include gifts given by the faithful in the form of money or other things for the sake of charity toward the poor. Moreover, external gifts must always be a visible expression of that true gift that God expects from us: a contrite heart, the love of God and neighbor by which we are conformed

---

147 Cf. ECUMENICAL COUNCIL OF TRENT, Session XXII, 17 September 1562, on the Most Holy Sacrifice of the Mass, Chapter 8: DS 1749; MISSALE ROMANUM, Institutio Generalis, no. 65.

148 Cf. POPE JOHN PAUL II, Allocution to a number of Bishops from the United States of America who had come to Rome for a visit "ad Limina Apostolorum," 28 May 1993, no. 2: AAS 86 (1994) p. 330.

149 Cf. Code of Canon Law, can. 386 §1.

to the sacrifice of Christ, who offered himself for us. For in the Eucharist, there shines forth most brilliantly that mystery of charity that Jesus brought forth at the Last Supper by washing the feet of the disciples. In order to preserve the dignity of the Sacred Liturgy, in any event, the external offerings should be brought forward in an appropriate manner. Money, therefore, just as other contributions for the poor, should be placed in an appropriate place which should be away from the eucharistic table.[150] Except for money and occasionally a minimal symbolic portion of other gifts, it is preferable that such offerings be made outside the celebration of Mass.

71. The practice of the Roman Rite is to be maintained according to which the peace is extended shortly before Holy Communion. For according to the tradition of the Roman Rite, this practice does not have the connotation either of reconciliation or of a remission of sins, but instead signifies peace, communion and charity before the reception of the Most Holy Eucharist.[151] It is rather the Penitential Act to be carried out at the beginning of Mass (especially in its first form) which has the character of reconciliation among brothers and sisters.

72. It is appropriate "that each one give the sign of peace only to those who are nearest and in a sober manner." "The Priest may give the sign of peace to the ministers but always remains within the sanctuary, so as not to disturb the celebration. He does likewise if for a just reason he wishes to extend the sign of peace to some few of the faithful." "As regards the sign to be exchanged, the manner is to be established by the Conference of Bishops in accordance with the dispositions and customs of the people," and their acts are subject to the *recognitio* of the Apostolic See.[152]

---

150   Cf. MISSALE ROMANUM, Institutio Generalis, no. 73.
151   Cf. ibid., no. 154.
152   Cf. ibid., nos. 82, 154.

73. In the celebration of Holy Mass the breaking of the Eucharistic Bread—done only by the Priest celebrant, if necessary with the help of a Deacon or of a concelebrant—begins after the exchange of peace, while the *Agnus Dei* is being recited. For the gesture of breaking bread "carried out by Christ at the Last Supper, which in apostolic times gave the whole eucharistic action its name, signifies that the faithful, though they are many, are made one Body in the communion of the one Bread of Life who is Christ, who died and rose for the world's salvation" (cf. 1 Cor 10:17).[153] For this reason the Rite must be carried out with great reverence.[154] Even so, it should be brief. The abuse that has prevailed in some places, by which this Rite is unnecessarily prolonged and given undue emphasis, with laypersons also helping in contradiction to the norms, should be corrected with all haste.[155]

74. If the need arises for the gathered faithful to be given instruction or testimony by a layperson in a church concerning the Christian life, it is altogether preferable that this be done outside Mass. Nevertheless, for serious reasons it is permissible that this type of instruction or testimony be given after the Priest has proclaimed the Prayer After Communion. This should not become a regular practice, however. Furthermore, these instructions and testimony should not be of such a nature that they could be confused with the homily,[156] nor is it permissible to dispense with the homily on their account.

---

153   Cf. ibid., no. 83.

154   Cf. S. CONGREGATION FOR DIVINE WORSHIP, Instruction, *Liturgicae instaurationes*, no. 5: AAS 62 (1970) p. 699.

155   Cf. MISSALE ROMANUM, Institutio Generalis, nos. 83, 240, 321.

156   Cf. CONGREGATION FOR THE CLERGY ET AL., Instruction, *Ecclesiae de mysterio*, Practical Provisions, article 3 §2: AAS 89 (1997) p. 865.

4. ON THE JOINING OF VARIOUS RITES WITH THE CELEBRATION OF MASS

75. On account of the theological significance inherent in a particular Rite and the Eucharistic Celebration, the liturgical books sometimes prescribe or permit the celebration of Holy Mass to be joined with another Rite, especially one of those pertaining to the Sacraments.[157] The Church does not permit such a conjoining in other cases, however, especially when it is a question of trivial matters.

76. Furthermore, according to a most ancient tradition of the Roman Church, it is not permissible to unite the Sacrament of Penance to the Mass in such a way that they become a single liturgical celebration. This does not exclude, however, that Priests other than those celebrating or concelebrating the Mass might hear the confessions of the faithful who so desire, even in the same place where Mass is being celebrated, in order to meet the needs of those faithful.[158] This should nevertheless be done in an appropriate manner.

77. The celebration of Holy Mass is not to be inserted in any way into the setting of a common meal, nor joined with this kind of banquet. Mass is not to be celebrated without grave necessity on a dinner table[159]

---

157 Cf. especially the *General Instruction of the Liturgy of the Hours*, nos. 93-98; ROMAN RITUAL, revised by decree of the Second Vatican Ecumenical Council and published by authority of Pope John Paul II: Book of Blessings, editio typica, 31 May 1984, General Introduction, no. 28; Order of Crowning an Image of the Blessed Virgin Mary, editio typica, 25 March 1981, nos. 10 and 14; S. CONGREGATION FOR DIVINE WORSHIP, Instruction on Masses with Particular Groups, *Actio pastoralis*, 15 May 1969: AAS 61 (1969) pp. 806-811; Directory for Masses with Children, Pueros baptizatos, 1 November 1973: AAS 66 (1974) pp. 30-46; MISSALE ROMANUM, Institutio Generalis, no. 21.

158 Cf. POPE JOHN PAUL II, Apostolic Letter (Motu Proprio), *Misericordia Dei*, 7 April 2002, no. 2: AAS 94 (2002) p. 455; Cf. CONGREGATION FOR DIVINE WORSHIP AND THE DISCIPLINE OF THE SACRAMENTS, Response to Dubium: *Notitiae* 37 (2001) pp. 259-260.

159 Cf. S. CONGREGATION FOR DIVINE WORSHIP, Instruction, *Liturgicae instaurationes*, no. 9: AAS 62 (1970) p. 702.

nor in a dining room or banquet hall, nor in a room where food is present, nor in a place where the participants during the celebration itself are seated at tables. If out of grave necessity Mass must be celebrated in the same place where eating will later take place, there is to be a clear interval of time between the conclusion of Mass and the beginning of the meal, and ordinary food is not to be set before the faithful during the celebration of Mass.

78. It is not permissible to link the celebration of Mass to political or secular events, nor to situations that are not fully consistent with the Magisterium of the Catholic Church. Furthermore, it is altogether to be avoided that the celebration of Mass should be carried out merely out of a desire for show, or in the manner of other ceremonies including profane ones, lest the Eucharist should be emptied of its authentic meaning.

79. Finally, it is strictly to be considered an abuse to introduce into the celebration of Holy Mass elements that are contrary to the prescriptions of the liturgical books and taken from the rites of other religions.

CHAPTER IV
Holy Communion

1. DISPOSITIONS FOR THE
RECEPTION OF HOLY COMMUNION

80. The Eucharist is to be offered to the faithful, among other reasons, "as an antidote, by which we are freed from daily faults and preserved from mortal sins,"[160] as is brought to light in various parts of the Mass. As for the Penitential Act placed at the beginning of Mass, it has the purpose of preparing all to be ready to celebrate the sacred mysteries;[161] even so, "it lacks the efficacy of the Sacrament of Penance,"[162] and cannot be regarded as a substitute for the Sacrament of Penance in remission of graver sins. Pastors of souls should take care to ensure diligent catechetical instruction, so that Christian doctrine is handed on to Christ's faithful in this matter.

81. The Church's custom shows that it is necessary for each person to examine himself at depth,[163] and that anyone who is conscious of grave sin should not celebrate or receive the Body of the Lord without prior sacramental confession, except for grave reason when the possibility of confession is lacking; in this case he will remember that he is bound by

---

160   ECUMENICAL COUNCIL OF TRENT, Session XIII, 11 October 1551, Decree on the Most Holy Eucharist, Chapter 2: DS 1638; cf. Session XXII, 17 September 1562, On the Most Holy Sacrifice of the Mass, Chapters 1-2: DS 1740, 1743; S. CONGREGATION OF RITES, Instruction, *Eucharisticum mysterium*, no. 35: AAS 59 (1967) p. 560.

161   Cf. MISSALE ROMANUM, Ordo Missae, no. 4, p. 505.

162   MISSALE ROMANUM, Institutio Generalis, no. 51.

163   Cf. 1 Cor 11:28.

the obligation of making an act of perfect contrition, which includes the intention to confess as soon as possible."[164]

82. Moreover, "the Church has drawn up norms aimed at fostering the frequent and fruitful access of the faithful to the Eucharistic table and at determining the objective conditions under which Communion may not be given."[165]

83. It is certainly best that all who are participating in the celebration of Holy Mass with the necessary dispositions should receive Communion. Nevertheless, it sometimes happens that Christ's faithful approach the altar as a group indiscriminately. It pertains to the Pastors prudently and firmly to correct such an abuse.

84. Furthermore when Holy Mass is celebrated for a large crowd—for example, in large cities—care should be taken lest out of ignorance non-Catholics or even non-Christians come forward for Holy Communion, without taking into account the Church's Magisterium in matters pertaining to doctrine and discipline. It is the duty of Pastors at an opportune moment to inform those present of the authenticity and the discipline that are strictly to be observed.

85. Catholic ministers licitly administer the Sacraments only to the Catholic faithful, who likewise receive them licitly only from Catholic ministers, except for those situations for which provision is made in

---

164   Cf. *Code of Canon Law*, can. 916; cf. ECUMENICAL COUNCIL OF TRENT, Session XIII, 11 October 1551, Decree on the Most Holy Eucharist, Chapter 7: DS 1646-1647; POPE JOHN PAUL II, Encyclical Letter, *Ecclesia de Eucharistia*, no. 36: AAS 95 (2003) pp. 457-458; S. CONGREGATION OF RITES, Instruction, *Eucharisticum mysterium*, no. 35: AAS 59 (1967) p. 561.

165   Cf. POPE JOHN PAUL II, Encyclical Letter, *Ecclesia de Eucharistia*, no. 42: AAS 95 (2003) p. 461.

canon 844 §§2, 3, and 4, and canon 861 §2.[166] In addition, the conditions comprising canon 844 §4, from which no dispensation can be given,[167] cannot be separated; thus, it is necessary that all of these conditions be present together.

86. The faithful should be led insistently to the practice whereby they approach the Sacrament of Penance outside the celebration of Mass, especially at the scheduled times, so that the Sacrament may be administered in a manner that is tranquil and truly beneficial to them, so as not to be prevented from active participation at Mass. Those who are accustomed to receiving Communion often or daily should be instructed that they should approach the Sacrament of Penance at appropriate intervals, in accordance with the condition of each.[168]

87. The First Communion of children must always be preceded by sacramental confession and absolution.[169] Moreover First Communion should always be administered by a Priest and never outside the celebration of Mass. Apart from exceptional cases, it is not particularly appropriate for First Communion to be administered on Holy Thursday of the Lord's Supper. Another day should be chosen instead, such as a

---

166 Cf. *Code of Canon Law*, can. 844 §1; POPE JOHN PAUL II, Encyclical Letter, *Ecclesia de Eucharistia*, nos. 45-46: AAS 95 (2003) pp. 463-464; cf. also PONTIFICAL COUNCIL FOR THE PROMOTION OF CHRISTIAN UNITY, Directory for the application of the principles and norms on ecumenism, *La recherche de l'unité*, nos. 130-131: AAS 85 (1993) pp. 1039-1119, here p. 1089.

167 Cf. POPE JOHN PAUL II, Encyclical Letter, *Ecclesia de Eucharistia*, no. 46: AAS 95 (2003) pp. 463-464.

168 Cf. S. CONGREGATION OF RITES, Instruction, *Eucharisticum mysterium*, no. 35: AAS 59 (1967) p. 561.

169 Cf. *Code of Canon Law*, can. 914; S. CONGREGATION FOR THE DISCIPLINE OF THE SACRAMENTS, Declaration, *Sanctus Pontifex*, 24 May 1973: AAS 65 (1973) p. 410; S. CONGREGATION FOR THE SACRAMENTS AND DIVINE WORSHIP and S. CONGREGATION FOR THE CLERGY, Letter to the Presidents of the Bishops' Conferences, *In quibusdam*, 31 March 1977: *Enchiridion Documentorum Instaurationis Liturgicae*, II, pp. 142-144; S. CONGREGATION FOR THE SACRAMENTS AND DIVINE WORSHIP and S. CONGREGATION FOR THE CLERGY, Response to dubium, 20 May 1977: AAS 69 (1977) p. 427.

Sunday between the Second and the Sixth Sunday of Easter, or the Solemnity of the Body and Blood of Christ, or the Sundays of Ordinary Time, since Sunday is rightly regarded as the day of the Eucharist.[170] "Children who have not attained the age of reason, or those whom" the Parish Priest "has determined to be insufficiently prepared" should not come forward to receive the Holy Eucharist.[171] Where it happens, however, that a child who is exceptionally mature for his age is judged to be ready for receiving the Sacrament, the child must not be denied First Communion provided he has received sufficient instruction.

2. THE DISTRIBUTION OF HOLY COMMUNION

88. The faithful should normally receive sacramental Communion of the Eucharist during Mass itself, at the moment laid down by the Rite of celebration, that is to say, just after the Priest celebrant's Communion.[172] It is the Priest celebrant's responsibility to minister Communion, perhaps assisted by other Priests or Deacons; and he should not resume the Mass until after the Communion of the faithful is concluded. Only when there is a necessity may extraordinary ministers assist the Priest celebrant in accordance with the norm of law.[173]

89. "So that even by means of the signs Communion may stand out more clearly as a participation in the Sacrifice being celebrated,"[174] it is

---

170 Cf. POPE JOHN PAUL II, Apostolic Letter, *Dies Domini*, 31 May 1998, nos. 31-34: AAS 90 (1998) pp. 713-766, here pp. 731-734.

171 Cf. *Code of Canon Law*, can. 914.

172 Cf. SECOND VATICAN ECUMENICAL COUNCIL, Constitution on the Sacred Liturgy, *Sacrosanctum Concilium*, no. 55.

173 Cf. S. CONGREGATION OF RITES, Instruction, *Eucharisticum mysterium*, no. 31: AAS 59 (1967) p. 558; PONTIFICAL COMMISSION FOR THE AUTHENTIC INTERPRETATION OF THE CODE OF CANON LAW, Response to dubium, 1 June 1988: AAS 80 (1988) p. 1373.

174 MISSALE ROMANUM, Institutio Generalis, no. 85.

preferable that the faithful be able to receive hosts consecrated in the same Mass.[175]

90. "The faithful should receive Communion kneeling or standing, as the Conference of Bishops will have determined," with its acts having received the *recognitio* of the Apostolic See. "However, if they receive Communion standing, it is recommended that they give due reverence before the reception of the Sacrament, as set forth in the same norms."[176]

91. In distributing Holy Communion it is to be remembered that "sacred ministers may not deny the sacraments to those who seek them in a reasonable manner, are rightly disposed, and are not prohibited by law from receiving them."[177] Hence any baptized Catholic who is not prevented by law must be admitted to Holy Communion. Therefore, it is not licit to deny Holy Communion to any of Christ's faithful solely on the grounds, for example, that the person wishes to receive the Eucharist kneeling or standing.

92. Although each of the faithful always has the right to receive Holy Communion on the tongue, at his choice,[178] if any communicant should wish to receive the Sacrament in the hand, in areas where the Bishops' Conference with the *recognitio* of the Apostolic See has given permission, the sacred host is to be administered to him or her. However, special care should be taken to ensure that the host is consumed by the communicant in the presence of the minister, so that no one goes away carrying the

---

175 Cf. SECOND VATICAN ECUMENICAL COUNCIL, Constitution on the Sacred Liturgy, *Sacrosanctum Concilium*, no. 55; S. CONGREGATION OF RITES, Instruction, *Eucharisticum mysterium*, no. 31: AAS 59 (1967) p. 558; MISSALE ROMANUM, Institutio Generalis, nos. 85, 157, 243.

176 Cf. MISSALE ROMANUM, Institutio Generalis, no. 160.

177 *Code of Canon Law*, can. 843 §1; cf. can. 915.

178 Cf. MISSALE ROMANUM, Institutio Generalis, no. 161.

Eucharistic species in his hand. If there is a risk of profanation, then Holy Communion should not be given in the hand to the faithful.[179]

93. The Communion-plate for the Communion of the faithful should be retained, so as to avoid the danger of the sacred host or some fragment of it falling.[180]

94. It is not licit for the faithful "to take . . . by themselves . . . and, still less, to hand . . . from one to another" the sacred host or the sacred chalice.[181] Moreover, in this regard, the abuse is to be set aside whereby spouses administer Holy Communion to each other at a Nuptial Mass.

95. A lay member of Christ's faithful "who has already received the Most Holy Eucharist may receive it again on the same day only within a Eucharistic Celebration in which he or she is participating, with due regard for the prescriptions of canon 921 § 2."[182]

96. The practice is reprobated whereby either unconsecrated hosts or other edible or inedible things are distributed during the celebration of Holy Mass or beforehand after the manner of Communion, contrary to the prescriptions of the liturgical books. For such a practice in no way accords with the tradition of the Roman Rite, and carries with it the danger of causing confusion among Christ's faithful concerning the Eucharistic doctrine of the Church. Where there exists in certain places by concession a particular custom of blessing bread after Mass for distribution, proper catechesis should very carefully be given concerning this action. In fact, no other similar practices should be introduced, nor should unconsecrated hosts ever be used for this purpose.

---

179 CONGREGATION FOR DIVINE WORSHIP AND THE DISCIPLINE OF THE SACRAMENTS, Dubium: *Notitiae* 35 (1999) pp. 160-161.
180 Cf. MISSALE ROMANUM, Institutio Generalis, no. 118.
181 Ibid., no. 160.
182 Cf. *Code of Canon Law*, can. 917; PONTIFICAL COMMISSION FOR THE AUTHENTIC INTERPRETATION OF THE CODE OF CANON LAW, Response to Dubium, 11 July 1984: AAS 76 (1984) p. 746.

3. THE COMMUNION OF PRIESTS

97. A Priest must communicate at the altar at the moment laid down by the Missal each time he celebrates Holy Mass, and the concelebrants must communicate before they proceed with the distribution of Holy Communion. The Priest celebrant or a concelebrant is never to wait until the people's Communion is concluded before receiving Communion himself.[183]

98. The Communion of Priest concelebrants should proceed according to the norms prescribed in the liturgical books, always using hosts consecrated at the same Mass[184] and always with Communion under both kinds being received by all of the concelebrants. It is to be noted that if the Priest or Deacon hands the sacred host or chalice to the concelebrants, he says nothing; that is to say, he does not pronounce the words "The Body of Christ" or "The Blood of Christ."

99. Communion under both kinds is always permitted "to Priests who are not able to celebrate or concelebrate Mass."[185]

4. COMMUNION UNDER BOTH KINDS

100. So that the fullness of the sign may be made more clearly evident to the faithful in the course of the Eucharistic banquet, lay members of Christ's faithful, too, are admitted to Communion under both kinds, in the cases set forth in the liturgical books, preceded and continually accompanied by proper catechesis regarding the dogmatic principles on this matter laid down by the Ecumenical Council of Trent.[186]

---

183 Cf. SECOND VATICAN ECUMENICAL COUNCIL, Constitution on the Sacred Liturgy, *Sacrosanctum Concilium*, no. 55; MISSALE ROMANUM, Institutio Generalis, nos. 158-160, 243-244, 246.

184 Cf. MISSALE ROMANUM, Institutio Generalis, nos. 237-249; cf. also nos. 85, 157.

185 Cf. ibid., no. 283a.

186 Cf. ECUMENICAL COUNCIL OF TRENT, Session XXI, 16 July 1562, Decree on Eucharistic Communion, Chapters 1-3: DS 1725-1729; SECOND VATICAN ECUMENICAL COUNCIL, Constitution on the Sacred Liturgy, *Sacrosanctum Concilium*, no. 55; MISSALE ROMANUM, Institutio Generalis, nos. 282-283.

101. In order for Holy Communion under both kinds to be administered to the lay members of Christ's faithful, due consideration should be given to the circumstances, as judged first of all by the diocesan Bishop. It is to be completely excluded where even a small danger exists of the sacred species being profaned.[187] With a view to wider coordination, the Bishops' Conferences should issue norms, once their decisions have received the *recognitio* of the Apostolic See through the Congregation for Divine Worship and the Discipline of the Sacraments, especially as regards "the manner of distributing Holy Communion to the faithful under both kinds, and the faculty for its extension."[188]

102. The chalice should not be ministered to lay members of Christ's faithful where there is such a large number of communicants[189] that it is difficult to gauge the amount of wine for the Eucharist and there is a danger that "more than a reasonable quantity of the Blood of Christ remain to be consumed at the end of the celebration."[190] The same is true wherever access to the chalice would be difficult to arrange, or where such a large amount of wine would be required that its certain provenance and quality could only be known with difficulty, or wherever there is not an adequate number of sacred ministers or extraordinary ministers of Holy Communion with proper formation, or where a notable part of the people continues to prefer not to approach the chalice for various reasons, so that the sign of unity would in some sense be negated.

103. The norms of the Roman Missal admit the principle that in cases where Communion is administered under both kinds, "the Blood of the Lord may be received either by drinking from the chalice directly, or by

---

187   Cf. MISSALE ROMANUM, Institutio Generalis, no. 283.
188   Cf. ibid.
189   Cf. S. CONGREGATION FOR DIVINE WORSHIP, Instruction, *Sacramentali Communione*, 29 June 1970: AAS 62 (1970) p. 665; Instruction, *Liturgicae instaurationes*, no. 6a: AAS 62 (1970) p. 699.
190   MISSALE ROMANUM, Institutio Generalis, no. 285a.

intinction, or by means of a tube or a spoon."[191] As regards the administering of Communion to lay members of Christ's faithful, the Bishops may exclude Communion with the tube or the spoon where this is not the local custom, though the option of administering Communion by intinction always remains. If this modality is employed, however, hosts should be used which are neither too thin nor too small, and the communicant should receive the Sacrament from the Priest only on the tongue.[192]

104. The communicant must not be permitted to intinct the host himself in the chalice, nor to receive the intincted host in the hand. As for the host to be used for the intinction, it should be made of valid matter, also consecrated; it is altogether forbidden to use non-consecrated bread or other matter.

105. If one chalice is not sufficient for Communion to be distributed under both kinds to the Priest concelebrants or Christ's faithful, there is no reason why the Priest celebrant should not use several chalices.[193] For it is to be remembered that all Priests in celebrating Holy Mass are bound to receive Communion under both kinds. It is praiseworthy, by reason of the sign value, to use a main chalice of larger dimensions, together with smaller chalices.

106. However, the pouring of the Blood of Christ after the consecration from one vessel to another is completely to be avoided, lest anything should happen that would be to the detriment of so great a mystery. Never to be used for containing the Blood of the Lord are flagons, bowls, or other vessels that are not fully in accord with the established norms.

107. In accordance with what is laid down by the canons, "one who throws away the consecrated species or takes them away or keeps them

---

191   Ibid., no. 245.
192   Cf. ibid., nos. 285b, 287.
193   Cf. ibid., nos. 207, 285a.

for a sacrilegious purpose, incurs a *latae sententiae* excommunication reserved to the Apostolic See; a cleric, moreover, may be punished by another penalty, not excluding dismissal from the clerical state."[194] To be regarded as pertaining to this case is any action that is voluntarily and gravely disrespectful of the sacred species. Anyone, therefore, who acts contrary to these norms, for example casting the sacred species into the sacrarium or in an unworthy place or on the ground, incurs the penalties laid down.[195] Furthermore all will remember that once the distribution of Holy Communion during the celebration of Mass has been completed, the prescriptions of the Roman Missal are to be observed, and in particular, whatever may remain of the Blood of Christ must be entirely and immediately consumed by the Priest or by another minister, according to the norms, while the consecrated hosts that are left are to be consumed by the Priest at the altar or carried to the place for the reservation of the Eucharist.[196]

---

194   Cf. *Code of Canon Law*, can. 1367.
195   Cf. PONTIFICAL COUNCIL FOR THE INTERPRETATION OF LEGISLATIVE TEXTS, Response to dubium, 3 July 1999: AAS 91 (1999) p. 918.
196   Cf. MISSALE ROMANUM, Institutio Generalis, nos. 163, 284.

CHAPTER V
Certain Other Matters Concerning the Eucharist

1. THE PLACE FOR THE CELEBRATION OF HOLY MASS

108. "The celebration of the Eucharist is to be carried out in a sacred place, unless in a particular case necessity requires otherwise. In this case the celebration must be in a decent place."[197] The diocesan Bishop shall be the judge for his diocese concerning this necessity, on a case-by-case basis.

109. It is never lawful for a Priest to celebrate in a temple or sacred place of any non-Christian religion.

2. VARIOUS CIRCUMSTANCES RELATING TO THE MASS

110. "Remembering always that in the mystery of the Eucharistic Sacrifice the work of redemption is constantly being carried out, Priests should celebrate frequently. Indeed, daily celebration is earnestly recommended, because, even if it should not be possible to have the faithful present, the celebration is an act of Christ and of the Church, and in carrying it out, Priests fulfill their principal role."[198]

---

197   *Code of Canon Law*, can. 932 §1; S. CONGREGATION FOR DIVINE WORSHIP, Instruction, *Liturgicae instaurationes*, no. 9: AAS 62 (1970) p. 701.

198   *Code of Canon Law*, can. 904; cf. SECOND VATICAN ECUMENICAL COUNCIL, Dogmatic Constitution on the Church, *Lumen gentium*, no. 3; Decree on the Ministry and Life of Priests, *Presbyterorum ordinis*, no. 13; cf. also ECUMENICAL COUNCIL OF TRENT, Session XXII, 17 September 1562, On the Most Holy Sacrifice of the Mass, Chapter 6: DS 1747; Pope Paul Pp. VI, Encyclical Letter *Mysterium fidei*, 3 September 1965: AAS 57 (1965) pp. 753-774, here pp. 761-762; cf. POPE JOHN PAUL II, Encyclical Letter, *Ecclesia de Eucharistia*, no. 11: AAS 95 (2003) pp. 440-441; S. CONGREGATION OF RITES, Instruction, *Eucharisticum mysterium*, no. 44: AAS 59 (1967) p. 564; MISSALE ROMANUM, Institutio Generalis, no. 19.

111. A Priest is to be permitted to celebrate or concelebrate the Eucharist "even if he is not known to the rector of the church, provided he presents commendatory letters" (i.e., a *celebret*) not more than a year old from the Holy See or his Ordinary or Superior "or unless it can be prudently judged that he is not impeded from celebrating."[199] Let the Bishops take measures to put a stop to any contrary practice.

112. Mass is celebrated either in Latin or in another language, provided that liturgical texts are used which have been approved according to the norm of law. Except in the case of celebrations of the Mass that are scheduled by the ecclesiastical authorities to take place in the language of the people, Priests are always and everywhere permitted to celebrate Mass in Latin.[200]

113. When Mass is concelebrated by several Priests, a language known both to all the concelebrating Priests and to the gathered people should be used in the recitation of the Eucharist Prayer. Where it happens that some of the Priests who are present do not know the language of the celebration and therefore are not capable of pronouncing the parts of the Eucharistic Prayer proper to them, they should not concelebrate, but instead should attend the celebration in choral dress in accordance with the norms.[201]

114. "At Sunday Masses in parishes, insofar as parishes are 'Eucharistic communities,' it is customary to find different groups, movements, associations, and even the smaller religious communities present in the parish."[202] While it is permissible that Mass should be

---

199   Cf. *Code of Canon Law*, can. 903; MISSALE ROMANUM, Institutio Generalis, no. 200.
200   Cf. SECOND VATICAN ECUMENICAL COUNCIL, Constitution on the Sacred Liturgy, *Sacrosanctum Concilium*, no. 36 §1; *Code of Canon Law*, can. 928.
201   Cf. MISSALE ROMANUM, Institutio Generalis, no. 114.
202   POPE JOHN PAUL II, Apostolic Letter, *Dies Domini*, no. 36: AAS 90 (1998) p. 735; cf. also S. CONGREGATION OF RITES, Instruction, *Eucharisticum mysterium*, no. 27: AAS 59 (1967) p. 556.

celebrated for particular groups according to the norm of law,[203] these groups are nevertheless not exempt from the faithful observance of the liturgical norms.

115. The abuse is reprobated by which the celebration of Holy Mass for the people is suspended in an arbitrary manner contrary to the norms of the Roman Missal and the healthy tradition of the Roman Rite, on the pretext of promoting a "fast from the Eucharist."

116. Masses are not to be multiplied contrary to the norm of law, and as regards Mass stipends, all those things are to be observed which are otherwise laid down by law.[204]

3. SACRED VESSELS

117. Sacred vessels for containing the Body and Blood of the Lord must be made in strict conformity with the norms of tradition and of the liturgical books.[205] The Bishops' Conferences have the faculty to decide whether it is appropriate, once their decisions have been given the *recognitio* by the Apostolic See, for sacred vessels to be made of other solid materials as well. It is strictly required, however, that such materials be truly noble in the common estimation within a given region,[206] so that honor will be given to the Lord by their use, and all risk of diminishing the doctrine of the Real Presence of Christ in the Eucharistic species in the eyes of the faithful will be avoided. Reprobated, therefore, is any practice of using for the celebration of Mass common vessels, or others lacking in quality, or devoid of all artistic merit or which are mere containers, as also other vessels made

---

203   Cf. POPE JOHN PAUL II, Apostolic Letter, *Dies Domini*, esp. no. 36: AAS 90 (1998) pp. 713-766, here pp. 735-736; S. Congregation for Divine Worship, Instruction, *Actio pastoralis*: AAS 61 (1969) pp. 806-811.

204   Cf. *Code of Canon Law*, cann. 905, 945-958; cf. CONGREGATION FOR THE CLERGY, Decree, *Mos iugiter*, 22 February 1991: AAS 83 (1991), pp. 443-446.

205   Cf. MISSALE ROMANUM, Institutio Generalis, nos. 327-333.

206   Cf. ibid., no. 332.

from glass, earthenware, clay, or other materials that break easily. This norm is to be applied even as regards metals and other materials that easily rust or deteriorate.[207]

118. Before they are used, sacred vessels are to be blessed by a Priest according to the Rites laid down in the liturgical books.[208] It is praiseworthy for the blessing to be given by the diocesan Bishop, who will judge whether the vessels are worthy of the use to which they are destined.

119. The Priest, once he has returned to the altar after the distribution of Communion, standing at the altar or at the credence table, purifies the paten or ciborium over the chalice, then purifies the chalice in accordance with the prescriptions of the Missal and wipes the chalice with the purificator. Where a Deacon is present, he returns with the Priest to the altar and purifies the vessels. It is permissible, however, especially if there are several vessels to be purified, to leave them, covered as may be appropriate, on a corporal on the altar or on the credence table, and for them to be purified by the Priest or Deacon immediately after Mass once the people have been dismissed. Moreover a duly instituted acolyte assists the Priest or Deacon in purifying and arranging the sacred vessels either at the altar or the credence table. In the absence of a Deacon, a duly instituted acolyte carries the sacred vessels to the credence table and there purifies, wipes and arranges them in the usual way.[209]

---

207   Cf. ibid., no. 332; CONGREGATION FOR DIVINE WORSHIP AND THE DISCIPLINE OF THE SACRAMENTS, Instruction, *Inaestimabile donum*, no. 16: AAS 72 (1980) p. 338.

208   Cf. MISSALE ROMANUM, Institutio Generalis, no. 333; Appendix IV, *Ordo benedictionis calicis et patenae intra Missam adhibendus*, pp. 1255-1257; PONTIFICALE ROMANUM EX DECRETO SACROSANCTI OECUMENICI CONCILII VATICANI II INSTAURATUM, AUCTORITATE PAULI PP. VI PROMULGATUM, Ordo Dedicationis ecclesiae et altaris, editio typica, 29 May 1977, Typis Polyglottis Vaticanis, 1977, Chapter VII, pp. 125-132.

209   Cf. MISSALE ROMANUM, Institutio Generalis, nos. 163, 183, 192.

120. Let Pastors take care that the linens for the sacred table, especially those which will receive the sacred species, are always kept clean and that they are washed in the traditional way. It is praiseworthy for this to be done by pouring the water from the first washing, done by hand, into the church's sacrarium or into the ground in a suitable place. After this a second washing can be done in the usual way.

4. LITURGICAL VESTURE

121. "The purpose of a variety of color of the sacred vestments is to give effective expression even outwardly to the specific character of the mysteries of faith being celebrated and to a sense of Christian life's passage through the course of the liturgical year."[210] On the other hand, the variety "of offices in the celebration of the Eucharist is shown outwardly by the diversity of sacred vestments. In fact, these "sacred vestments should also contribute to the beauty of the sacred action itself."[211]

122. "The alb" is "to be tied at the waist with a cincture unless it is made so as to fit even without a cincture. Before the alb is put on, if it does not completely cover the ordinary clothing at the neck, an amice should be put on."[212]

123. "The vestment proper to the Priest celebrant at Mass, and in other sacred actions directly connected with Mass unless otherwise indicated, is the chasuble, worn over the alb and stole."[213] Likewise the Priest, in putting on the chasuble according to the rubrics, is not to omit the stole. All Ordinaries should be vigilant in order that all usage to the contrary be eradicated.

---

210   Ibid., no. 345.
211   Ibid., no. 335.
212   Cf. ibid., no. 336.
213   Cf. ibid., no. 337.

124. A faculty is given in the Roman Missal for the Priest concelebrants at Mass other than the principal concelebrant (who should always put on a chasuble of the prescribed color), for a just reason such as a large number of concelebrants or a lack of vestments, to omit "the chasuble, using the stole over the alb."[214] Where a need of this kind can be foreseen, however, provision should be made for it insofar as possible. Out of necessity the concelebrants other than the principal celebrant may even put on white chasubles. For the rest, the norms of the liturgical books are to be observed.

125. The proper vestment of the Deacon is the dalmatic, to be worn over an alb and stole. In order that the beautiful tradition of the Church may be preserved, it is praiseworthy to refrain from exercising the option of omitting the dalmatic.[215]

126. The abuse is reprobated whereby the sacred ministers celebrate Holy Mass or other Rites without sacred vestments or with only a stole over the monastic cowl or the common habit of religious or ordinary clothes, contrary to the prescriptions of the liturgical books, even when there is only one minister participating.[216] In order that such abuses be corrected as quickly as possible, Ordinaries should take care that in all churches and oratories subject to their jurisdiction there is present an adequate supply of liturgical vestments made in accordance with the norms.

127. A special faculty is given in the liturgical books for using sacred vestments that are festive or more noble on more solemn occasions, even if they are not of the color of the day.[217] However, this faculty, which is specifically intended in reference to vestments made many

---

214   Cf. ibid., no. 209.
215   Cf. ibid., no. 338.
216   Cf. S. Congregation for Divine Worship, Instruction, *Liturgicae instaurationes*, no. 8c: AAS 62 (1970) p. 701.
217   Cf. Missale Romanum, Institutio Generalis, no. 346g.

years ago, with a view to preserving the Church's patrimony, is improperly extended to innovations by which forms and colors are adopted according to the inclination of private individuals, with disregard for traditional practice, while the real sense of this norm is lost to the detriment of the tradition. On the occasion of a feastday, sacred vestments of a gold or silver color can be substituted as appropriate for others of various colors, but not for purple or black.

128. Holy Mass and other liturgical celebrations, which are acts of Christ and of the People of God hierarchically constituted, are ordered in such a way that the sacred ministers and the lay faithful manifestly take part in them each according to his own condition. It is preferable therefore that "Priests who are present at a Eucharistic Celebration, unless excused for a good reason, should as a rule exercise the office proper to their Order and thus take part as concelebrants, wearing the sacred vestments. Otherwise, they wear their proper choir dress or a surplice over a cassock."[218] It is not fitting, except in rare and exceptional cases and with reasonable cause, for them to participate at Mass, as regards to externals, in the manner of the lay faithful.

---

218   Ibid., no. 114; cf. nos. 16-17.

CHAPTER VI
The Reservation of the Most Holy Eucharist and Eucharistic Worship Outside Mass

1. THE RESERVATION OF THE MOST HOLY EUCHARIST

129. "The celebration of the Eucharist in the Sacrifice of the Mass is truly the origin and end of the worship given to the Eucharist outside the Mass. Furthermore the sacred species are reserved after Mass principally so that the faithful who cannot be present at Mass, above all the sick and those advanced in age, may be united by sacramental Communion to Christ and his Sacrifice which is offered in the Mass."[219] In addition, this reservation also permits the practice of adoring this great Sacrament and offering it the worship due to God. Accordingly, forms of adoration that are not only private but also public and communitarian in nature, as established or approved by the Church herself, must be greatly promoted.[220]

130. "According to the structure of each church building and in accordance with legitimate local customs, the Most Holy Sacrament is to be reserved in a tabernacle in a part of the church that is noble, prominent, readily visible, and adorned in a dignified manner" and furthermore "suitable for prayer" by reason of the quietness of the location, the space available in front of the tabernacle, and also the supply of benches or

---

219 S. Congregation for Divine Worship, Decree, *Eucharistiae sacramentum*, 21 June 1973: AAS 65 (1973) p. 610.

220 Cf. ibid.

seats and kneelers.[221] In addition, diligent attention should be paid to all the prescriptions of the liturgical books and to the norm of law,[222] especially as regards the avoidance of the danger of profanation.[223]

131. Apart from the prescriptions of canon 934 §1, it is forbidden to reserve the Blessed Sacrament in a place that is not subject in a secure way to the authority of the diocesan Bishop, or where there is a danger of profanation. Where such is the case, the diocesan Bishop should immediately revoke any permission for reservation of the Eucharist that may already have been granted.[224]

132. No one may carry the Most Holy Eucharist to his or her home, or to any other place contrary to the norm of law. It should also be borne in mind that removing or retaining the consecrated species for a sacrilegious purpose or casting them away are *graviora delicta*, the absolution of which is reserved to the Congregation for the Doctrine of the Faith.[225]

133. A Priest or Deacon, or an extraordinary minister who takes the Most Holy Eucharist when an ordained minister is absent or impeded

---

221   Cf. S. CONGREGATION OF RITES, Instruction, *Eucharisticum mysterium*, no. 54: AAS 59 (1967) p. 568; Instruction, *Inter Oecumenici*, 26 September 1964, no. 95: AAS 56 (1964) pp. 877-900, here p. 898; MISSALE ROMANUM, Institutio Generalis, no. 314.

222   Cf. POPE JOHN PAUL II, Letter, *Dominicae Cenae*, no. 3: AAS 72 (1980) pp. 117-119; S. CONGREGATION OF RITES, Instruction, *Eucharisticum mysterium*, no. 53: AAS 59 (1967) p. 568; *Code of Canon Law*, can. 938 §2; ROMAN RITUAL, *Holy Communion and Worship of the Eucharist Outside Mass*, Introduction, no. 9; MISSALE ROMANUM, Institutio Generalis, nos. 314-317.

223   Cf. *Code of Canon Law*, can. 938 §§3-5.

224   S. CONGREGATION FOR THE DISCIPLINE OF THE SACRAMENTS, Instruction, *Nullo unquam*, 26 May 1938, no. 10d: AAS 30 (1938) pp. 198-207, here p. 206.

225   Cf. POPE JOHN PAUL II, Apostolic Letter (Motu Proprio), *Sacramentorum sanctitatis tutela*, 30 April 2001: AAS 93 (2001) pp. 737-739; CONGREGATION FOR THE DOCTRINE OF THE FAITH, Ep. ad totius Catholicae Ecclesiae Episcopos aliosque Ordinarios et Hierarchas quorum interest: de delictis gravioribus eidem Congregationi pro Doctrina Fidei reservatis: AAS 93 (2001) p. 786.

in order to administer it as Communion for a sick person, should go insofar as possible directly from the place where the Sacrament is reserved to the sick person's home, leaving aside any profane business so that any danger of profanation may be avoided and the greatest reverence for the Body of Christ may be ensured. Furthermore the Rite for the administration of Communion to the sick, as prescribed in the Roman Ritual, is always to be used.[226]

2. CERTAIN FORMS OF WORSHIP OF THE
MOST HOLY EUCHARIST OUTSIDE MASS

134. "The worship of the Eucharist outside the Sacrifice of the Mass is a tribute of inestimable value in the life of the Church. Such worship is closely linked to the celebration of the Eucharistic Sacrifice."[227] Therefore both public and private devotion to the Most Holy Eucharist even outside Mass should be vigorously promoted, for by means of it the faithful give adoration to Christ, truly and really present,[228] the "High Priest of the good things to come"[229] and Redeemer of the whole world. "It is the responsibility of sacred Pastors, even by the witness of their life, to support the practice of Eucharistic worship and especially exposition of the Most Holy Sacrament, as well as prayer of adoration before Christ present under the eucharistic species."[230]

---

226   Cf. ROMAN RITUAL, Holy Communion and Worship of the Eucharist Outside Mass, nos. 26-78.

227   Pope John Paul II, Encyclical Letter, Ecclesia de Eucharistia, no. 25: AAS 95 (2003) pp. 449-450.

228   Cf. ECUMENICAL COUNCIL OF TRENT, Session XIII, 11 October 1551, Decree on the Most Holy Eucharist, Chapter 5: DS 1643; POPE PIUS XII, Encyclical Letter, Mediator Dei: AAS 39 (1947) p. 569; POPE PAUL VI, Encyclical Letter, Mysterium Fidei, 3 September 1965: AAS 57 (1965) pp. 751-774, here pp. 769-770; S. CONGREGATION OF RITES, Instruction, Eucharisticum mysterium, no. 3f: AAS 59 (1967) p. 543; S. CONGREGATION FOR THE SACRAMENTS AND DIVINE WORSHIP, Instruction, Inaestimabile donum, no. 20: AAS 72 (1980) p. 339; POPE JOHN PAUL II, Encyclical Letter, Ecclesia de Eucharistia, no. 25: AAS 95 (2003) pp. 449-450.

229   Cf. Heb 9:11; POPE JOHN PAUL II, Encyclical Letter, Ecclesia de Eucharistia, no. 3: AAS 95 (2003) p. 435.

230   POPE JOHN PAUL II, Encyclical Letter, Ecclesia de Eucharistia, no. 25: AAS 95 (2003) p. 450.

135. The faithful "should not omit making visits during the day to the Most Holy Sacrament, as a proof of gratitude, a pledge of love, and a debt of the adoration due to Christ the Lord who is present in it."[231] For the contemplation of Jesus present in the Most Holy Sacrament, as a communion of desire, powerfully joins the faithful to Christ, as is splendidly evident in the example of so many Saints.[232] "Unless there is a grave reason to the contrary, a church in which the Most Holy Eucharist is reserved should be open to the faithful for at least some hours each day, so that they can spend time in prayer before the Most Holy Sacrament."[233]

136. The Ordinary should diligently foster Eucharistic adoration, whether brief or prolonged or almost continuous, with the participation of the people. For in recent years in so many places "adoration of the Most Holy Sacrament is also an important daily practice and becomes an inexhaustible source of holiness," although there are also places "where there is evident almost a total lack of regard for worship in the form of eucharistic adoration."[234]

137. Exposition of the Most Holy Eucharist must always be carried out in accordance with the prescriptions of the liturgical books.[235] Before the Most Holy Sacrament either reserved or exposed, the praying of the Rosary, which is admirable "in its simplicity and even its profundity," is not to be excluded either.[236] Even so, especially if there

---

231   POPE PAUL VI, Encyclical Letter, *Mysterium fidei*: AAS 57 (1965) p. 771.

232   Cf. POPE JOHN PAUL II, Encyclical Letter, *Ecclesia de Eucharistia*, no. 25: AAS 95 (2003) pp. 449-450.

233   *Code of Canon Law*, can. 937.

234   POPE JOHN PAUL II, Encyclical Letter, *Ecclesia de Eucharistia*, no. 10: AAS 95 (2003) p. 439.

235   Cf. ROMAN RITUAL, Holy Communion and Worship of the Eucharist Outside Mass, nos. 82-100; MISSALE ROMANUM, Institutio Generalis, no. 317; *Code of Canon Law*, can. 941 §2.

236   POPE JOHN PAUL II, Apostolic Letter, *Rosarium Virginis Mariae*, 16 October 2002: AAS 95 (2003) pp. 5-36, here no. 2, p. 6.

is Exposition, the character of this kind of prayer as a contemplation of the mystery of the life of Christ the Redeemer and the Almighty Father's design of salvation should be emphasized, especially by making use of readings taken from Sacred Scripture.[237]

138. Still, the Most Holy Sacrament, when exposed, must never be left unattended even for the briefest space of time. It should therefore be arranged that at least some of the faithful always be present at fixed times, even if they take alternating turns.

139. Where the diocesan Bishop has sacred ministers or others whom he can assign to this purpose, the faithful have a right to visit the Most Holy Sacrament of the Eucharist frequently for adoration, and to take part in adoration before the Most Holy Eucharist exposed at least at some time in the course of any given year.

140. It is highly recommended that at least in the cities and the larger towns the diocesan Bishop should designate a church building for perpetual adoration; in it, however, Holy Mass should be celebrated frequently, even daily if possible, while the Exposition should rigorously be interrupted while Mass is being celebrated.[238] It is fitting that the host to be exposed for adoration should be consecrated in the Mass immediately preceding the time of adoration, and that it should be placed in the monstrance upon the altar after Communion.[239]

---

237   Cf. CONGREGATION FOR DIVINE WORSHIP AND THE DISCIPLINE OF THE SACRAMENTS, Letter of the Congregation, 15 January 1997: *Notitiae* 34 (1998) pp. 506-510; APOSTOLIC PENITENTIARY, Letter to a Priest, 8 March 1996: *Notitiae* 34 (1998) p. 511.

238   Cf. S. CONGREGATION OF RITES, Instruction, *Eucharisticum mysterium*, no. 61: AAS 59 (1967) p. 571; ROMAN RITUAL, Holy Communion and Worship of the Eucharist Outside Mass, no. 83; MISSALE ROMANUM, Institutio Generalis, no. 317; *Code of Canon Law,* can. 941 §2.

239   Cf. ROMAN RITUAL, Holy Communion and Worship of the Eucharist Outside Mass, no. 94.

141. The diocesan Bishop should acknowledge and foster insofar as possible the right of the various groups of Christ's faithful to form guilds or associations for the carrying out of adoration, even almost continuous adoration. Whenever such associations assume an international character, it pertains to the Congregation for Divine Worship and the Discipline of the Sacraments to erect them and to approve their statutes.[240]

3. EUCHARISTIC CONGRESSES AND EUCHARISTIC PROCESSIONS

142. "It is for the diocesan Bishop to establish regulations about processions in order to provide for participation in them and for their being carried out in a dignified way"[241] and to promote adoration by the faithful.

143. "Wherever it is possible in the judgment of the diocesan Bishop, a procession through the public streets should be held, especially on the Solemnity of the Body and Blood of Christ as a public witness of reverence for the Most Holy Sacrament,"[242] for the "devout participation of the faithful in the eucharistic procession on the Solemnity of the Body and Blood of Christ is a grace from the Lord which yearly fills with joy those who take part in it."[243]

---

240 Cf. POPE JOHN PAUL II, Apostolic Constitution, *Pastor bonus*, article 65: AAS 80 (1988) p. 877.

241 *Code of Canon Law*, can. 944 §2; cf. ROMAN RITUAL, Holy Communion and Worship of the Eucharist Outside Mass, Introduction, no. 102; MISSALE ROMANUM, Institutio Generalis, no. 317.

242 *Code of Canon Law*, can. 944 §1; cf. ROMAN RITUAL, Holy Communion and Worship of the Eucharist Outside Mass, Introduction, nos. 101-102; MISSALE ROMANUM, Institutio Generalis, no. 317.

243 *Pope John Paul* II, Encyclical Letter, *Ecclesia de Eucharistia*, no. 10: AAS 95 (2003) p. 439.

144. Although this cannot be done in some places, the tradition of holding Eucharistic processions should not be allowed to be lost. Instead, new ways should be sought of holding them in today's conditions: for example, at shrines, or in public gardens if the civil authority agrees.

145. The pastoral value of Eucharistic Congresses should be highly esteemed, and they "should be a genuine sign of faith and charity."[244] Let them be diligently prepared and carried out in accordance with what has been laid down,[245] so that Christ's faithful may have the occasion to worship the sacred mysteries of the Body and Blood of the Son of God in a worthy manner, and that they may continually experience within themselves the fruits of the Redemption.[246]

---

244 Cf. ROMAN RITUAL, Holy Communion and Worship of the Eucharist Outside Mass, Introduction, no. 109.
245 Cf. ibid., nos. 109-112.
246 Cf. MISSALE ROMANUM, In sollemnitate sanctissimi Corporis et Sanguinis Christi, Collecta, p. 489.

CHAPTER VII
Extraordinary Functions of
Lay Faithful

146. There can be no substitute whatsoever for the ministerial Priesthood. For if a Priest is lacking in the community, then the community lacks the exercise and sacramental function of Christ the Head and Shepherd, which belongs to the essence of its very life.[247] For "the only minister who can confect the sacrament of the Eucharist *in persona Christi* is a validly ordained Priest."[248]

147. When the Church's needs require it, however, if sacred ministers are lacking, lay members of Christ's faithful may supply for certain liturgical offices according to the norm of law.[249] Such faithful are called and appointed to carry out certain functions, whether of greater or lesser weight, sustained by the Lord's grace. Many of the lay Christian faithful have already contributed eagerly to this service and still do so, especially in missionary areas where the Church is still of

---

247 Cf. CONGREGATION FOR THE CLERGY ET AL., Instruction, *Ecclesiae de mysterio*, Theological Principles, no. 3: AAS 89 (1997) p. 859.

248 Cf. *Code of Canon Law*, can. 900 §1; cf. FOURTH LATERAN ECUMENICAL COUNCIL, 11-30 November 1215, Chapter 1: DS 802; POPE CLEMENT VI, Letter to Mekhitar, Catholicos of the Armenians, *Super quibusdam*, 29 September 1351: DS 1084; ECUMENICAL COUNCIL OF TRENT, Session XXIII, 15 July 1563, Doctrine and Canons on Sacred Orders, Chapter 4: DS 1767-1770; POPE PIUS XII, Encyclical Letter, *Mediator Dei*: AAS 39 (1947) p. 553.

249 Cf. *Code of Canon Law*, can. 230 §3; POPE JOHN PAUL II, Allocution during a Symposium concerning the collaboration of laypersons in the pastoral ministry of Priests, 22 April 1994, no. 2: *L'Osservatore Romano*, 23 April 1994; CONGREGATION FOR THE CLERGY ET AL., Instruction, *Ecclesiae de mysterio*, Prooemium: AAS 89 (1997) pp. 852-856.

small dimensions or is experiencing conditions of persecution,[250] but also in areas affected by a shortage of Priests and Deacons.

148. Particular importance is to be attached to the training of catechists, who by means of great labors have given and still give outstanding and altogether necessary help in the spreading of the Faith and of the Church.[251]

149. More recently, in some dioceses long since evangelized, members of Christ's lay faithful have been appointed as "pastoral assistants," and among them many have undoubtedly served the good of the Church by providing assistance to the Bishop, Priests and Deacons in the carrying out of their pastoral activity. Let care be taken, however, lest the delineation of this function be assimilated too closely to the form of pastoral ministry that belongs to clerics. That is to say, attention should be paid to ensuring that "pastoral assistants" do not take upon themselves what is proper to the ministry of the sacred ministers.

150. The activity of a pastoral assistant should be directed to facilitating the ministry of Priests and Deacons, to ensuring that vocations to the Priesthood and Diaconate are awakened and that lay members of Christ's faithful in each community are carefully trained for the various liturgical functions, in keeping with the variety of charisms and in accordance with the norm of law.

151. Only out of true necessity is there to be recourse to the assistance of extraordinary ministers in the celebration of the Liturgy. Such recourse is not intended for the sake of a fuller participation of the laity

---

250   Cf. POPE JOHN PAUL II, Encyclical Letter, *Redemptoris missio*, nos. 53-54: AAS 83 (1991) pp. 300-302; CONGREGATION FOR THE CLERGY ET AL., Instruction, *Ecclesiae de mysterio*, Prooemium: AAS 89 (1997) pp. 852-856.

251   Cf. SECOND VATICAN ECUMENICAL COUNCIL, Decree on the Missionary Activity of the Church, *Ad gentes*, 7 December 1965, no. 17; POPE JOHN PAUL II, Encyclical Letter, *Redemptoris missio*, no. 73: AAS 83 (1991) p. 321.

but rather, by its very nature, is supplementary and provisional.[252] Furthermore, when recourse is had out of necessity to the functions of extraordinary ministers, special urgent prayers of intercession should be multiplied that the Lord may soon send a Priest for the service of the community and raise up an abundance of vocations to sacred Orders.[253]

152. These purely supplementary functions must not be an occasion for disfiguring the very ministry of Priests, in such a way that the latter neglect the celebration of Holy Mass for the people for whom they are responsible, or their personal care of the sick, or the Baptism of children, or assistance at weddings or the celebration of Christian funerals, matters which pertain in the first place to Priests assisted by Deacons. It must therefore never be the case that in parishes Priests alternate indiscriminately in shifts of pastoral service with Deacons or laypersons, thus confusing what is specific to each.

153. Furthermore, it is never licit for laypersons to assume the role or the vesture of a Priest or a Deacon or other clothing similar to such vesture.

1. THE EXTRAORDINARY MINISTER OF HOLY COMMUNION

154. As has already been recalled, "the only minister who can confect the Sacrament of the Eucharist in persona Christi is a validly ordained Priest."[254] Hence the name "minister of the Eucharist" belongs properly to the Priest alone. Moreover, also by reason of their sacred Ordination, the ordinary ministers of Holy Communion are the Bishop, the Priest and the Deacon,[255] to whom it belongs therefore to

---

252 Cf. CONGREGATION FOR THE CLERGY ET AL., Instruction, *Ecclesiae de mysterio*, Practical Provisions, art. 8 §2: AAS 89 (1997) p. 872.

253 Cf. POPE JOHN PAUL II, Encyclical Letter, *Ecclesia de Eucharistia*, no. 32: AAS 95 (2003) p. 455.

254 Cf. *Code of Canon Law*, can. 900 §1.

255 Cf. ibid., can. 910 §1; cf. also POPE JOHN PAUL II, Letter, *Dominicae Cenae*, no. 11: AAS 72 (1980) p. 142; CONGREGATION FOR THE CLERGY ET AL., Instruction, *Ecclesiae de mysterio*, Practical Provisions, article 8 §1: AAS 89 (1997) pp. 870-871.

administer Holy Communion to the lay members of Christ's faithful during the celebration of Mass. In this way their ministerial office in the Church is fully and accurately brought to light, and the sign value of the Sacrament is made complete.

155. In addition to the ordinary ministers there is the formally instituted acolyte, who by virtue of his institution is an extraordinary minister of Holy Communion even outside the celebration of Mass. If, moreover, reasons of real necessity prompt it, another lay member of Christ's faithful may also be delegated by the diocesan Bishop, in accordance with the norm of law,[256] for one occasion or for a specified time, and an appropriate formula of blessing may be used for the occasion. This act of appointment, however, does not necessarily take a liturgical form, nor, if it does take a liturgical form, should it resemble sacred Ordination in any way. Finally, in special cases of an unforeseen nature, permission can be given for a single occasion by the Priest who presides at the celebration of the Eucharist.[257]

156. This function is to be understood strictly according to the name by which it is known, that is to say, that of extraordinary minister of Holy Communion, and not "special minister of Holy Communion" nor "extraordinary minister of the Eucharist" nor "special minister of the Eucharist," by which names the meaning of this function is unnecessarily and improperly broadened.

---

256 Cf. *Code of Canon Law*, can. 230 §3.

257 Cf. S. CONGREGATION FOR THE DISCIPLINE OF THE SACRAMENTS, Instruction, *Immensae caritatis*, prooemium: AAS 65 (1973) p. 264; POPE PAUL VI, Apostolic Letter (Motu Proprio), *Ministeria quaedam*, 15 August 1972: AAS 64 (1972) p. 532; MISSALE ROMANUM, Appendix III: Ritus ad deputandum ministrum sacrae Communionis ad actum distribuendae, p. 1253; CONGREGATION FOR THE CLERGY ET AL., Instruction, *Ecclesiae de mysterio*, Practical Provisions, article 8 §1: AAS 89 (1997) p. 871.

157. If there is usually present a sufficient number of sacred ministers for the distribution of Holy Communion, extraordinary ministers of Holy Communion may not be appointed. Indeed, in such circumstances, those who may have already been appointed to this ministry should not exercise it. The practice of those Priests is reprobated who, even though present at the celebration, abstain from distributing Communion and hand this function over to laypersons.[258]

158. Indeed, the extraordinary minister of Holy Communion may administer Communion only when the Priest and Deacon are lacking, when the Priest is prevented by weakness or advanced age or some other genuine reason, or when the number of faithful coming to Communion is so great that the very celebration of Mass would be unduly prolonged.[259] This, however, is to be understood in such a way that a brief prolongation, considering the circumstances and culture of the place, is not at all a sufficient reason.

159. It is never allowed for the extraordinary minister of Holy Communion to delegate anyone else to administer the Eucharist, as for example a parent or spouse or child of the sick person who is the communicant.

160. Let the diocesan Bishop give renewed consideration to the practice in recent years regarding this matter, and if circumstances call for it, let him correct it or define it more precisely. Where such extraordinary

---

258 S. CONGREGATION FOR THE SACRAMENTS AND DIVINE WORSHIP, Instruction, *Inaestimabile donum*, no. 10: AAS 72 (1980) p. 336; PONTIFICAL COMMISSION FOR THE AUTHENTIC INTERPRETATION OF THE CODE OF CANON LAW, Response to dubium, 11 July 1984: AAS 76 (1984) p. 746.

259 Cf. S. CONGREGATION FOR THE DISCIPLINE OF THE SACRAMENTS, Instruction, *Immensae caritatis*, no. 1: AAS 65 (1973) pp. 264-271, here pp. 265-266; PONTIFICAL COMMISSION FOR THE AUTHENTIC INTERPRETATION OF THE CODE OF CANON LAW, Responsio ad propositum dubium, 1 June 1988: AAS 80 (1988) p. 1373; CONGREGATION FOR THE CLERGY ET AL., Instruction, *Ecclesiae de mysterio*, Practical Provisions, art. 8 §2: AAS 89 (1997) p. 871.

ministers are appointed in a widespread manner out of true necessity, the diocesan Bishop should issue special norms by which he determines the manner in which this function is to be carried out in accordance with the law, bearing in mind the tradition of the Church.

2. PREACHING

161. As was already noted above, the homily on account of its importance and its nature is reserved to the Priest or Deacon during Mass.[260] As regards other forms of preaching, if necessity demands it in particular circumstances, or if usefulness suggests it in special cases, lay members of Christ's faithful may be allowed to preach in a church or in an oratory outside Mass in accordance with the norm of law.[261] This may be done only on account of a scarcity of sacred ministers in certain places, in order to meet the need, and it may not be transformed from an exceptional measure into an ordinary practice, nor may it be understood as an authentic form of the advancement of the laity.[262] All must remember besides that the faculty for giving such permission belongs to the local Ordinary, and this as regards individual instances; this permission is not the competence of anyone else, even if they are Priests or Deacons.

3. PARTICULAR CELEBRATIONS CARRIED OUT IN THE ABSENCE OF A PRIEST

162. On the day known as the Lord's Day, the Church faithful gathers together to commemorate the Lord's Resurrection and the whole Paschal Mystery, especially by the celebration of Mass.[263] For "no Christian

---

260   Cf. *Code of Canon Law*, can. 767 §1.
261   Cf. ibid., can. 766.
262   Cf. CONGREGATION FOR THE CLERGY ET AL., Instruction, *Ecclesiae de mysterio*, Practical Provisions, article 2 §§3-4: AAS 89 (1997) p. 865.
263   Cf. POPE JOHN PAUL II, Apostolic Letter, *Dies Domini*, especially nos. 31-51: AAS 90 (1998) pp. 713-766, here pp. 731-746; POPE JOHN PAUL II, Apostolic Letter, *Novo Millennio ineunte*, 6 January 2001, nos. 35-36: AAS 93 (2001) pp. 290-292; POPE JOHN PAUL II, Encyclical Letter, *Ecclesia de Eucharistia*, no. 41: AAS 95 (2003) pp. 460-461.

community is built up unless it is rooted in and hinges upon the celebration of the Most Holy Eucharist."[264] Hence it is the Christian people's right to have the Eucharist celebrated for them on Sunday, and whenever holydays of obligation or other major feasts occur, and even daily insofar as this is possible. Therefore when it is difficult to have the celebration of Mass on a Sunday in a parish church or in another community of Christ's faithful, the diocesan Bishop together with his Priests should consider appropriate remedies.[265] Among such solutions will be that other Priests be called upon for this purpose, or that the faithful transfer to a church in a nearby place so as to participate in the Eucharistic mystery there.[266]

163. All Priests, to whom the Priesthood and the Eucharist are entrusted *for the sake of* others,[267] should remember that they are enjoined to provide the faithful with the opportunity to satisfy the obligation of participating at Mass on Sundays.[268] For their part, the lay faithful have the right, barring a case of real impossibility, that no Priest should ever refuse either to celebrate Mass for the people or to have it celebrated by another Priest if the people otherwise would not be able to satisfy the obligation of participating at Mass on Sunday or the other days of precept.

---

264 SECOND VATICAN ECUMENICAL COUNCIL, Decree on the Ministry and Life of Priests, *Presbyterorum ordinis*, no. 6; cf. POPE JOHN PAUL II, Encyclical Letter, *Ecclesia de Eucharistia*, nos. 22, 33: AAS 95 (2003) pp. 448, 455-456.

265 Cf. S. CONGREGATION OF RITES, Instruction, *Eucharisticum mysterium*, no. 26: AAS 59 (1967) pp. 555-556; CONGREGATION FOR DIVINE WORSHIP, Directory for Sunday Celebrations in the Absence of a Priest, *Christi Ecclesia*, 2 June 1988, nos. 5, 25: *Notitiae* 24 (1988) pp. 366-378, here pp. 367, 372.

266 Cf. CONGREGATION FOR DIVINE WORSHIP, Directory for Sunday Celebrations in the Absence of a Priest, *Christi Ecclesia*, no. 18: Notitiae 24 (1988) p. 370.

267 Cf. POPE JOHN PAUL II, Letter, *Dominicae Cenae*, no. 2: AAS 72 (1980) p. 116.

268 Cf. POPE JOHN PAUL II, Apostolic Letter, *Dies Domini*, no. 49: AAS 90 (1998) p. 744; Encyclical Letter, *Ecclesia de Eucharistia*, no. 41: AAS 95 (2003) pp. 460-461; *Code of Canon Law*, cann. 1246-1247.

164. "If participation at the celebration of the Eucharist is impossible on account of the absence of a sacred minister or for some other grave cause,"[269] then it is the Christian people's right that the diocesan Bishop should provide as far as he is able for some celebration to be held on Sundays for that community under his authority and according to the Church's norms. Sunday celebrations of this specific kind, however, are to be considered altogether extraordinary. All Deacons or lay members of Christ's faithful who are assigned a part in such celebrations by the diocesan Bishop should strive "to keep alive in the community a genuine 'hunger' for the Eucharist, so that no opportunity for the celebration of Mass will ever be missed, also taking advantage of the occasional presence of a Priest who is not impeded by Church law from celebrating Mass."[270]

165. It is necessary to avoid any sort of confusion between this type of gathering and the celebration of the Eucharist.[271] The diocesan Bishops, therefore, should prudently discern whether Holy Communion ought to be distributed in these gatherings. The matter would appropriately be determined in view of a more ample coordination in the Bishops' Conference, to be put into effect after the *recognitio* of the acts by the Apostolic See through the Congregation for Divine Worship and the Discipline of the Sacraments. It will be preferable, moreover, when both a Priest and a Deacon are absent, that the various parts be distributed among several faithful rather than having a single lay member of the faithful direct the whole celebration alone. Nor is it ever appropriate to refer to any member of the lay faithful as "presiding" over the celebration.

---

269   Cf. *Code of Canon Law*, can. 1248 §2; CONGREGATION FOR DIVINE WORSHIP, Directory for Sunday Celebrations in the Absence of a Priest, *Christi Ecclesia*, nos. 1-2: Notitiae 24 (1988) p. 366.

270   POPE JOHN PAUL II, Encyclical Letter, *Ecclesia de Eucharistia*, no. 33: AAS 95 (2003) pp. 455-456.

271   Cf. CONGREGATION FOR DIVINE WORSHIP, Directory for Sunday Celebrations in the Absence of a Priest, *Christi Ecclesia*, no. 22: *Notitiae* 24 (1988) p. 371.

166. Likewise, especially if Holy Communion is distributed during such celebrations, the diocesan Bishop, to whose exclusive competence this matter pertains, must not easily grant permission for such celebrations to be held on weekdays, especially in places where it was possible or would be possible to have the celebration of Mass on the preceding or the following Sunday. Priests are therefore earnestly requested to celebrate Mass daily for the people in one of the churches entrusted to their care.

167. "Similarly, it is unthinkable on the Lord's Day to substitute for Holy Mass either ecumenical celebrations of the word or services of common prayer with Christians from the . . . Ecclesial Communities, or even participation in these Communities' liturgical services."[272] Should the diocesan Bishop out of necessity authorize the participation of Catholics for a single occasion, let pastors take care lest confusion arise among the Catholic faithful concerning the necessity of taking part at Mass at another hour of the day even in such circumstances, on account of the obligation.[273]

4. THOSE WHO HAVE LEFT THE CLERICAL STATE

168. "A cleric who loses the clerical state in accordance with the law . . . is prohibited from exercising the power of order."[274] It is therefore not licit for him to celebrate the Sacraments under any pretext whatsoever

---

272 Pope John Paul II, Encyclical Letter, *Ecclesia de Eucharistia*, no. 30: AAS 95 (2003) pp. 453-454; cf. also Pontifical Council for the Promotion of Christian Unity, Directory for the application of the principles and norms on ecumenism, *La recherche de l'unité*, 25 March 1993, no. 115: AAS 85 (1993) pp. 1039-1119, here p. 1085.

273 Cf. Pontifical Council for the Promotion of Christian Unity, Directory for the application of the principles and norms on ecumenism, *La recherche de l'unité*, no. 115: AAS 85 (1993) p. 1085.

274 Cf. *Code of Canon Law*, can. 292; Pontifical Council for the Interpretation of Legislative Texts, Declaration de recta interpretatione can. 1335, secundae partis, CIC, 15 May 1997, no. 3: AAS 90 (1998) p. 64.

save in the exceptional case set forth by law,[275] nor is it licit for Christ's faithful to have recourse to him for the celebration, since there is no reason which would permit this according to canon 1335.[276] Moreover, these men should neither give the homily[277] nor ever undertake any office or duty in the celebration of the sacred Liturgy, lest confusion arise among Christ's faithful and the truth be obscured.

---

275   Cf. *Code of Canon Law*, cann. 976, 986 §2.

276   Cf. PONTIFICAL COUNCIL FOR THE INTERPRETATION OF LEGISLATIVE TEXTS, Declaratio de recta interpretatione can. 1335, secundae partis, CIC, 15 May 1997, nos. 1-2: AAS 90 (1998) pp. 63-64.

277   As regards Priests who have obtained the dispensation from celibacy, cf. S. CONGREGATION FOR THE DOCTRINE OF THE FAITH, Normae de dispensatione a sacerdotali caelibatu ad instantiam partis, *Normae substantiales*, 14 October 1980, article 5; cf. also CONGREGATION FOR THE CLERGY ET AL., Instruction, *Ecclesiae de mysterio*, Practical Provisions, article 3 §5: AAS 89 (1997) p. 865.

CHAPTER VIII
Remedies

169. Whenever an abuse is committed in the celebration of the Sacred Liturgy, it is to be seen as a real falsification of Catholic Liturgy. St. Thomas wrote, "The vice of falsehood is perpetrated by anyone who offers worship to God on behalf of the Church in a manner contrary to that which is established by the Church with divine authority, and to which the Church is accustomed."[278]

170. In order that a remedy may be applied to such abuses, "there is a pressing need for the biblical and liturgical formation of the People of God, both pastors and faithful,"[279] so that the Church's faith and discipline concerning the Sacred Liturgy may be accurately presented and understood. Where abuses persist, however, proceedings should be undertaken for safeguarding the spiritual patrimony and rights of the Church in accordance with the law, employing all legitimate means.

171. Among the various abuses there are some which are objectively *graviora delicta* or otherwise constitute grave matters, as well as others which are nonetheless to be carefully avoided and corrected. Bearing in mind everything that is treated especially in Chapter I of this Instruction, attention should be paid to what follows.

1. *GRAVIORA DELICTA*

172. *Graviora delicta* against the sanctity of the Most August Sacrifice and Sacrament of the Eucharist are to be handled in accordance with

---

278   St. Thomas Aquinas, *Summa Theol.*, II, 2, q. 93, a. 1.
279   Cf. Pope John Paul II, Apostolic Letter, *Vicesimus quintus annus*, no. 15: AAS 81 (1989) p. 911; cf. also Second Vatican Ecumenical Council, Constitution on the Sacred Liturgy, *Sacrosanctum Concilium*, nos. 15-19.

the *Norms Concerning* Graviora Delicta *Reserved to the Congregation for the Doctrine of the Faith*,[280] namely:

a. taking away or retaining the consecrated species for sacrilegious ends, or the throwing them away;[281]

b. the attempted celebration of the liturgical action of the Eucharistic Sacrifice or the simulation of the same;[282]

c. the forbidden concelebration of the Eucharistic Sacrifice with ministers of Ecclesial Communities that do not have the apostolic succession nor acknowledge the sacramental dignity of priestly Ordination;[283]

d. the consecration for sacrilegious ends of one matter without the other in the celebration of the Eucharist or even of both outside the celebration of the Eucharist.[284]

---

280 Cf. POPE JOHN PAUL II, Apostolic Letter (Motu Proprio), *Sacramentorum sanctitatis tutela*: AAS 93 (2001) pp. 737-739; CONGREGATION FOR THE DOCTRINE OF THE FAITH, Ep. ad totius Catholicae Ecclesiae Episcopos aliosque Ordinarios et Hierarchas quorum interest: de delictis gravioribus eidem Congregationi pro Doctrina Fidei reservatis: AAS 93 (2001) p. 786.

281 Cf. *Code of Canon Law*, can. 1367; PONTIFICAL COUNCIL FOR THE INTERPRETATION OF LEGISLATIVE TEXTS, Responsio ad propositum dubium, 3 July 1999: AAS 91 (1999) p. 918; CONGREGATION FOR THE DOCTRINE OF THE FAITH, Ep. ad totius Catholicae Ecclesiae Episcopos aliosque Ordinarios et Hierarchas quorum interest: De delictis gravioribus eidem Congregationi pro Doctrina Fidei reservatis: AAS 93 (2001) p. 786.

282 Cf. *Code of Canon Law*, cann. 1378 §2°1, 1379; CONGREGATION FOR THE DOCTRINE OF THE FAITH, Ep. ad totius Catholicae Ecclesiae Episcopos aliosque Ordinarios et Hierarchas quorum interest: De delictis gravioribus eidem Congregationi pro Doctrina Fidei reservatis: AAS 93 (2001) p. 786.

283 Cf. *Code of Canon Law*, cann. 908, 1365; CONGREGATION FOR THE DOCTRINE OF THE FAITH, Ep. ad totius Catholicae Ecclesiae Episcopos aliosque Ordinarios et Hierarchas quorum interest: De delictis gravioribus eidem Congregationi pro Doctrina Fidei reservatis: AAS 93 (2001) p. 786.

284 Cf. *Code of Canon Law*, can. 927; CONGREGATION FOR THE DOCTRINE OF THE FAITH, Ep. ad totius Catholicae Ecclesiae Episcopos aliosque Ordinarios et Hierarchas quorum interest: De delictis gravioribus eidem Congregationi pro Doctrina Fidei reservatis: AAS 93 (2001) p. 786.

2. GRAVE MATTERS

173. Although the gravity of a matter is to be judged in accordance with the common teaching of the Church and the norms established by her, objectively to be considered among grave matters is anything that puts at risk the validity and dignity of the Most Holy Eucharist: namely, anything that contravenes what is set out above in nos. 48-52, 56, 76-77, 79, 91-92, 94, 96, 101-102, 104, 106, 109, 111, 115, 117, 126, 131-133, 138, 153 and 168. Moreover, attention should be given to the other prescriptions of the *Code of Canon Law*, and especially what is laid down by canons 1364, 1369, 1373, 1376, 1380, 1384, 1385, 1386, and 1398.

3. OTHER ABUSES

174. Furthermore, those actions that are brought about which are contrary to the other matters treated elsewhere in this Instruction or in the norms established by law are not to be considered of little account, but are to be numbered among the other abuses to be carefully avoided and corrected.

175. The things set forth in this Instruction obviously do not encompass all the violations against the Church and its discipline that are defined in the canons, in the liturgical laws and in other norms of the Church for the sake of the teaching of the Magisterium or sound tradition. Where something wrong has been committed, it is to be corrected according to the norm of law.

4. THE DIOCESAN BISHOP

176. The diocesan Bishop, "since he is the principal dispenser of the mysteries of God, is to strive constantly so that Christ's faithful entrusted to his care may grow in grace through the celebration of the sacraments, and that they may know and live the Paschal Mystery."[285]

---

285   *Code of Canon Law*, can. 387.

It is his responsibility, "within the limits of his competence, to issue norms on liturgical matters by which all are bound."[286]

177. "Since he must safeguard the unity of the universal Church, the Bishop is bound to promote the discipline common to the entire Church and therefore to insist upon the observance of all ecclesiastical laws. He is to be watchful lest abuses encroach upon ecclesiastical discipline, especially as regards the ministry of the Word, the celebration of the Sacraments and sacramentals, the worship of God and the veneration of the Saints."[287]

178. Hence whenever a local Ordinary or the Ordinary of a religious Institute or of a Society of apostolic life receives at least a plausible notice of a delict or abuse concerning the Most Holy Eucharist, let him carefully investigate, either personally or by means of another worthy cleric, concerning the facts and the circumstances as well as the imputability.

179. Delicts against the Faith as well as *graviora delicta* committed in the celebration of the Eucharist and the other Sacraments are to be referred without delay to the Congregation for the Doctrine of the Faith, which "examines them and, if necessary, proceeds to the declaration or imposition of canonical sanctions according to the norm of common or proper law."[288]

180. Otherwise the Ordinary should proceed according to the norms of the sacred canons, imposing canonical penalties if necessary, and bearing in mind in particular that which is laid down by canon 1326. If the matter is serious, let him inform the Congregation for Divine Worship and the Discipline of the Sacraments.

286　Ibid., can. 838 §4.
287　Ibid., can. 392.
288　Cf. POPE JOHN PAUL II, Apostolic Constitution, *Pastor bonus*, article 52: AAS 80 (1988) p. 874.

5. THE APOSTOLIC SEE

181. Whenever the Congregation for Divine Worship and the Discipline of the Sacraments receives at least a plausible notice of a delict or an abuse concerning the Most Holy Eucharist, it informs the Ordinary so that he may investigate the matter. When the matter turns out to be serious, the Ordinary should send to the same Dicastery as quickly as possible a copy of the acts of the inquiry that has been undertaken, and where necessary, the penalty imposed.

182. In more difficult cases the Ordinary, for the sake of the good of the universal Church in the care for which he too has a part by virtue of his sacred Ordination, should not fail to handle the matter, having previously taken advice from the Congregation for Divine Worship and the Discipline of the Sacraments. For its part, this Congregation, on the strength of the faculties given to it by the Roman Pontiff, according to the nature of the case, will assist the Ordinary, granting him the necessary dispensations[289] or giving him instructions or prescriptions, which he is to follow diligently.

6. COMPLAINTS REGARDING
ABUSES IN LITURGICAL MATTERS

183. In an altogether particular manner, let everyone do all that is in their power to ensure that the Most Holy Sacrament of the Eucharist will be protected from any and every irreverence or distortion and that all abuses be thoroughly corrected. This is a most serious duty incumbent upon each and every one, and all are bound to carry it out without any favoritism.

---

289   Cf. ibid., no. 63: AAS 80 (1988) p. 876.

184. Any Catholic, whether Priest or Deacon or lay member of Christ's faithful, has the right to lodge a complaint regarding a liturgical abuse to the diocesan Bishop or the competent Ordinary equivalent to him in law, or to the Apostolic See on account of the primacy of the Roman Pontiff.[290] It is fitting, however, insofar as possible, that the report or complaint be submitted first to the diocesan Bishop. This is naturally to be done in truth and charity.

---

290   Cf. ibid.; cf. also *Code of Canon Law*, can. 1417 §1.

Conclusion

185. "Against the seeds of discord which daily experience shows to be so deeply ingrained in human nature as a result of sin, there stands the creative power of the unity of Christ's body. For it is precisely by building up the Church that the Eucharist establishes fellowship among men."[291] It is therefore the hope of this Congregation for Divine Worship and the Discipline of the Sacraments that also, by the diligent application of those things that are recalled in this Instruction, human weakness may come to pose less of an obstacle to the action of the Most Holy Sacrament of the Eucharist, and that with all distortion set aside and every reprobated practice removed,[292] through the intercession of the Blessed Virgin Mary, "Woman of the Eucharist," the saving presence of Christ in the Sacrament of his Body and Blood may shine brightly upon all people.

186. Let all Christ's faithful participate in the Most Holy Eucharist as fully, consciously and actively as they can,[293] honoring it lovingly by their devotion and the manner of their life. Let Bishops, Priests and Deacons, in the exercise of the sacred ministry, examine their consciences as regards the authenticity and fidelity of the actions they have performed in the name of Christ and the Church in the celebration of the Sacred Liturgy. Let each one of the sacred ministers ask himself, even with severity, whether he has respected the rights of the lay members of Christ's faithful, who confidently entrust themselves and their children to him, relying on him to fulfill for the faithful those sacred

---

291   Pope John Paul II, Encyclical Letter, *Ecclesia de Eucharistia*, no. 24: AAS 95 (2003) p. 449.

292   Cf. ibid., nos. 53-58: AAS 95 (2003) pp. 469-472.

293   Cf. Second Vatican Ecumenical Council, Constitution on the Sacred Liturgy, *Sacrosanctum Concilium*, no. 14; cf. also nos. 11, 41, 48.

functions that the Church intends to carry out in celebrating the Sacred Liturgy at Christ's command.[294] For each one should always remember that he is a servant of the Sacred Liturgy.[295]

All things to the contrary notwithstanding.

This Instruction, prepared by the Congregation for Divine Worship and the Discipline of the Sacraments by mandate of the Supreme Pontiff John Paul II in collaboration with the Congregation for the Doctrine of the Faith, was approved by the same Pontiff on the Solemnity of St. Joseph, March 19, 2004, and he ordered it to be published and to be observed immediately by all concerned.

From the offices of the Congregation for Divine Worship and the Discipline of the Sacraments, Rome, on the Solemnity of the Annunciation of the Lord, March 25, 2004.

Francis Cardinal Arinze
Prefect

+ Domenico Sorrentino
Archbishop Secretary

---

294   Cf. St. Thomas Aquinas, *Summa Theol.*, III, q. 64, a. 9 ad 1.
295   Cf. Missale Romanum, Institutio Generalis, no. 24.